Social Torment

Social Torment

Globalization in Atlantic Canada

W. Thom Workman

Fernwood Publishing • Halifax

Editing: Donna Davis
Cover art: Richard Slye
Design and production: Beverley Rach
Printed and bound in Canada by: Hignell Printing Limited

A publication of:
Fernwood Publishing
Site 2A, Box 5
8422 St. Margaret's Bay Road
Black Point, Nova Scotia
B0J 1B0

Fernwood Publishing Company Limited gratefully acknowledges the financial support of the Department of Canadian Heritage, the Nova Scotia Department of Tourism and Culture and the Canada Council for the Arts for our publishing program.

NOVA SCOTIA
Tourism and Culture

Le Conseil des Arts | The Canada Council
du Canada | for the Arts

National Library of Canada Cataloguing in Publication

Workman, W. Thom, 1959-
      Social torment: globalization in Atlantic Canada / Thom Workman.

Includes bibliographical references.
ISBN 1-55266-096-6

1. Globalization—Economic aspects—Atlantic Provinces.
2. Globalization—Social aspects—Atlantic Provinces. 3. Atlantic Provinces—Economic conditions—1991-. 4. Atlantic Provinces—Social conditions—1991-. I. Title.

HN110.A8W67 2002   330.9715'04   C2002-903646-1

Contents

List of Tables and Figures

Acknowledgements

There are many people who helped in the production of this brief study. I wish to acknowledge the inspirational role of the members of the *On the Table* editorial collective—Jean-Claude Basque, Bertrand Bégin, Carol Ferguson, David Frank, Rod Hill, Joan McFarland and Tom Steep. Their enthusiasm and spirited support for working people across the region helped things along in a way that is hard to express. Important forward movement was also made by the indefatigable efforts of John Murphy and Jean-Marie Nadeau of the New Brunswick Federation of Labour. Many others provided invaluable information and insights into the struggles of working people and the poor across the region, including Ian Johnson, Mary Boyd and Brian Curley.

I am indebted to the data librarians at the University of New Brunswick, Elizabeth Hamilton and Siobhan Hanratty, who patiently walked me through the wilderness of data at Statistics Canada, and who were kind enough to send in search parties when I routinely failed to emerge from the adventure. Two students at the University of New Brunswick, Brian Fodor and Andrea Foster, undertook some of the statistical work, and I am very grateful for their labours as I am for the proofreading done by Kirby Arbean and Melinda Kavanaugh. I also wish to thank Debbie Sloan, administrative secretary in the Department of Political Science at the University of New Brunswick, for her kind and patient support during the production of this manuscript.

A hearty thank you must go to Raymond Léger and David Bedford, also members of the *On the Table* collective, and friends and colleagues who took the time to peruse drafts of the manuscript and to provide helpful comments and feedback. This manuscript was vastly improved by the attentive copy-editing of Donna Davis, and especially by her helpful suggestions regarding its language and style. And there would be no manuscript at all were it not for the unwavering support of Errol Sharpe and the labours and assistance provided by Beverley Rach and Larissa Holman at Fernwood Publishing.

A special kind of thanks must also go to Meredith, Bronwyn and

Tristan, who, as children, desire to see their names in print and who thus like the fact that their father is a writer. Finally, I wish to say thank you—in print—to Beverly for providing encouragement, advice and guidance along such a bitter-sweet path.

To the many Atlantic Canadians who toil away for a non-living wage.

Preface

At the risk of sounding a bit downbeat, it is undeniable that our world is one of job losses, collapsing currencies, civil wars, protests, imperialist wars, more protests, urban-shock terrorism, chronic unemployment, refugee crises, sporadic factory occupations, still more protests, surreal contrasts in wealth and poverty, long and bitter strikes, falling real wages and so many other disturbing things that it simply boggles the mind. A Panglossian spin on the contemporary age is next to impossible. We witness so much anxiety, bitterness, cruelty, frustration and misery.

Many people set about, quite understandably, to make sense of it all. The suspicion persists that some of the bad things must be related, but connecting them is daunting. Countless reports, documentaries, journalistic essays, government studies, academic treatises, novels and poems try to process the things going on around us, but they almost invariably fail to connect events and developments in a satisfying and convincing way. The Archimidean standpoint eludes us. Still, such failures do not extinguish the sense that the issues dominating the nightly news are somehow related. A feeling of dissatisfaction with prevailing accounts of contemporary life loiters in our minds. A sort of double disillusionment sets in: one driven by the dispiriting events and developments in our world, and the other by the failure to satisfactorily account for the things unfolding before us.

This study tries to correct the second failing. It explicitly makes connections, connections that cluster around a simple observation: capital is rolling back the great class compromise forged in the middle part of the twentieth century. This class compact, forged by the resistance of working people many decades ago, has been unwinding everywhere. The deal is off, and for the last three decades capital has been engaged in a concerted drive to redefine the terms of the compact, and it is succeeding. Many of the seemingly disparate social, political and economic developments are connected to this orchestrated shift in the character of class relations.

Categories of understanding, inherited from previous epochs and

1

adjusted to suit our times, help us to draw these connections and to sift through the welter of change so that we can see the evolving struggle between classes in more or less certain terms. It is easy, however, to lose sight of the fundamentals of this analysis, to sacrifice its essential elements to an endless stream of contingencies. We fall prey to the belief that the critic—the "critical critic," as Marx put it in *The German Ideology*—should soothe the anxieties and calm the fears of today's activists and left politicians; we thoughtlessly celebrate every working-class triumph and despair over every working-class setback as though they marked the course of history; and in so doing ignore the solacing counsel of a more patient and reflective standpoint, which advises that the long-term survival of the capitalist system is no more conceivable now than it was a century and a half ago. Our world may not depart in a flash as was believed before the capitalist states refined the tools of war and propaganda, before the media took to the air and before the tapestry of contemporary culture thickened, but it will take leave just the same. This necessity is sunken into our world, a world that is negated, over and over on all fronts; it is not, nor can it be, a world at rest, not even for a moment. Its essential contradictions inexorably drive it ahead—to whatever.

And so it is possible to stand back and make sense of things. To the disciplined eye, recent history is not as open-ended, as random or, indeed, as "lost" as it might first appear. At this point, however, the urge to speak self-consciously is overwhelming. Identifying and reflecting on the essential orderliness of contemporary history leaves the analysis open to all sorts of fashionable charges. Rigorous scrutiny informed by an *epistēmē* is passé in this day and age. The intellectual milieu of contemporary life thrives on its capacity to expose the moment of "groundedness" in any formula or system, and it stands ready to deliver a mortal blow to grand narration. In effect, its accusations, not unlike those of the epistemological skeptics of earlier times who made the funny knowledge claim that there can be no knowledge, amount to the grandest narrative of all, but this much tends to be denied. As Hegel might have put it, in the last few decades it is less the case that reason has turned inwards to dwell upon its essence, and rather more the case that it has turned against itself in a paradoxical and very one-sided manner. The consequences of this dialogue have been very strange indeed; they also come at a most unfortunate moment. In a sense, the agonizing undulations of the class struggle have been doubly costly. For all that the scale of the human toll of the great roll-back has been staggering, the scope of the intellectual toll is almost as remarkable. In what some have called a "retreat," we have seen countless critics and naysayers numbed by an impressive array of intellectual opiates. In the process the ranks of reformers have swelled and the hearts of apologists have been gladdened. If I were from a family of capital, never seeing too far into the future, I would revel in the temper of contemporary intellectual life, for it poses no threat whatsoever.

Simply put, we (or should I facetiously say those of us who are "left") must not succumb to such tranquillizing darts. We have no business forsaking those who suffer so grievously at the hands of the globalizing capital. We will do well to remember that the sophists proper, the "sceptical skeptics" who dogged Socrates, Plato and so many others, have been around in every age and in many forms. As the class struggle grows older and greyer our task also becomes clearer, obligated as we are to dab a little colour here and a little colour there as we squint into the early evening sun.

Note on electronic sources

Many of the websites consulted during the research for this book were accessed, and research material drawn from them, on numerous occasions over the course of many months. During this time, some sites evolved and some URLs changed. The access dates listed in the bibliography reflect our most recent visits to the websites, most of which took place immediately prior to publishing and at which time the research material was available. We have made every effort to offer current, accessible website addresses.

Chapter 1

Unpacking Globalization

Atlantic Canada has been drawn into the new global economy, and the political consensus is that everything will keep getting better. "We are on the threshold of a new frontier," claimed New Brunswick Premier Bernard Lord in the fall of 2000, "of a new economy in which there are no borders. In which time and distance are no longer barriers." Lord added that the new economy had also advanced far beyond anything that our parents would have imagined:

> The knowledge-based economy and the application of informa-
> tion technologies that drive it present incredible opportunities,
> and challenges for all society. It is changing the way we do
> business, the way we communicate, the way we learn, and indeed,
> the way we live. (Lord 2000)

A few days later Nova Scotia premier John Hamm also emphasized the opportunities created by the new global economy: "Nova Scotia is getting better because the new information age and the new knowledge economy mean markets that were once far away and inaccessible ... are now within easy reach" (Hamm 2000).

According to political leaders in Atlantic Canada globalization offers hope and opportunity. Is this claim tenable? Is it something that Atlantic Canadians should embrace? To explore the impact of globalization on the region we must first make some sense about the widely used but poorly understood idea of globalization itself. This is a challenging requirement, especially since there is a sprawling commentary about globalization in intellectual and political circles. The term is used to explain the inability of governments to exercise certain policy options, to refer to specific changes in the world economy and to describe the inevitable destiny of humankind. In cutting through this woolly commentary it is helpful to observe that globalization leaves at least two marks upon the world. One is the exciting notion of "global village" with its glitz and glitter, including the internet, global money markets and liberalized trading regimes.

The second is the rise in hardship and anxiety among so many people around the world. This latter signature receives, at best, only passing attention in scholarly and popular commentary; it is an afterthought in the stories told by the vast majority of writers and economists. Such neglect alone demands that we position ourselves in a way to appreciate better the human suffering directly linked to globalization. We must acknowledge that behind its polished and flashy exterior are practices that create stunning hardship and misery for many of the world's people.

This account of globalization in terms of its growth in hardship has been undertold and, for the most part, silenced in the records of official-dom. Nevertheless, this is the account understood by those who bear the brunt of the globalization push. A more truthful portrait of global life does not have to circulate publicly to be known and widely appreciated by its victims. A richer and more rounded story about globalization, one that recognizes that its successes and achievements have been at the expense of vulnerable people around the world, will resound equally well with a young Malaysian woman toiling away in a semi-conductor facility and a single mother part-timing in a call centre in New Brunswick. Ironically, it is precisely this side of globalization neglected by pundits, journalists, intellectuals and politicians that Atlantic Canadians are more likely to experience. Although the region is increasingly plugged into the globaliz-ing world, the glamorous dimension of globalization is not as obvious in the region as it is elsewhere. Globalization does not sparkle in Nova Scotia or Prince Edward Island the way it does in Toronto, New York and Tokyo. It is commonplace to observe that the superconcentrations of wealth associated with globalization tend to be based in a handful of corporate conglomerates and the parasitic urbanized elite anchored to Northern mega-cities. In Atlantic Canada, in view of the relative concen-tration of riches outside the region, the telltale signs of obscene wealth— its proliferating pageantry, its conspicuous consumption, the explosion of private clubs and so on—tend not to be so glaring. But the same cannot be said for those who are being devoured by globalization. The intensifying exploitation of working people is spread out more evenly around the globe, and Atlantic Canadians are caught in this web. Globalization tends to unfold in the region in a more pedestrian fashion, with unnumbered employers of all sizes taking advantage of working people in a climate of austerity and a downshift in wages.

The working hunch in this study of Atlantic Canada is that what is good for globalization tends to be bad for people. There are not simply two sides to our new globalizing world—a good side that rewards some and a nasty side that harms so many others. Rather, the very achievements of globalization are premised on the mounting misery of its innumerable victims. The growing hardship imposed upon working people around the world is a necessary consequence of globalization; its glossy, outer shell merely makes this connection more difficult to see. Out of its accomplishments—the internet and high-tech gadgetry, dot-com economics, the emergence of the super-rich, the astonishing movement of goods and money, unprecedented levels of consumption, indulgences such as eco-tourism and psycho-therapy for family pets and so on—we can anticipate the growing wretchedness of much of the world's population. Unless we are to believe naïvely that leisure and luxury crystallize out of thin air, we must recognize and acknowledge that the comforts of globalization are reaped from the labour and toil of others. The only thing trickling down to the world's masses is more work and greater hardship. The impressive accomplishments of the last three decades are entwined with the deepening oppression of working people the world over. Despite the protestations of countless economists and politicians to the contrary, the fruits of the new world economy are not to be shared by everyone. Its beguiling comfort zones, zones that touch the owners of capital and extend to a wealthy managerial strata, high-end professionals and a legion of intellectuals ruminating away in designer personas, do not emerge out of the toil, sweat and, indeed, blood of those who enjoy them. One-sided sketches of globalization that celebrate its prosperity unforgivably trivialize the poverty and hardship of the vast majority of the world's people. Worse still, they cannot even begin to recognize the necessary link between the leisured life of the privileged few and the swelling ranks of the exhausted, the poor and the hungry.

To make sense of these related sides of globalization we must begin by recognizing that both its celebrated accomplishments and its undergrowth of human misery are wrapped up in the timeless class struggles endemic to capitalist societies. In its historically significant sense globalization is an episode in the ongoing struggle between the leaders of capital and working people throughout the world. It is this conflict that cradles globalization, and to cheat the language of the German philosopher G.W.F. Hegel a bit, this struggle is neither old or new, but rather eternal. Well over a century ago Karl Marx wrote at the outset of his influential *Communist Manifesto* that "the history of all hitherto existing society is the history of class struggles." As we navigate through the towering wealth and mounting misery of the last few decades we see the conflicts between owners and workers continuing to shape our world, just as the historic struggles between master and slave, lord and serf, and patrician and plebeian did so long ago. As William Greider (1997: 39) reminds us in his sweeping account of the global economy in the late-twentieth century, "The fundamental struggle, then as now, is between capital and labour. That struggle is always about control of the workplace and how the returns of the enterprise shall be divided."

With this conflict between capitalists and workers in mind, we can consider the nature of globalization by first seeing it as a strategy by large corporations—a strategy to enhance profitability by lowering production costs, especially wage costs. Globalization is a way to do things, a way to conduct business that works from the perspective of very large corporations. It is a campaign conceived in piecemeal fashion in boardrooms throughout North America, Europe and Japan and implemented by a countless number of corporate minions and managerial hirelings operating in every corner of the globe. The grand plan is formalized in business-funded think tanks and lobby groups, and the message is routinely conveyed to governments, politicians and journalists around the world. Globalization is a canalized tactic banked by capital on the one side and the world of working people on the other. It is conceived and formalized on high and then forced on working people around the globe. It amounts to the latest version of "best corporate practices" as we cross over into a new millennium.

It is not easy to see the strategic element of globalization in the welter of public parlance. Indeed, the sheer volume of commentary limits the likelihood that a clear sense of the term will emerge. Repeated exposure to the message that globalization is upon us is inescapable. Politicians remind us that globalization is the new fact of national life, and they identify it as the primary reason for introducing extraordinarily unpopular policies. The vague notion of a new world economy that no nation can sidestep also informs most political and social commentary in the media. And business leaders routinely claim that their short-term and long-term corporate decisions are guided by the exigencies of the global economy. Unfortunately, few of these discussions identify corporate-based, profit-driven motives as the primary force behind the globalization push, and even fewer still recognize the corporate imperative of driving down labour costs.

This lack of clarity is compounded by the plush rhetoric cloaking the idea of globalization. In popular discussion it is sometimes presented as the inexorable gravitation of humanity to a higher plane of existence. It is scarcely an exaggeration to say that globalization is frequently sold as the final moment in the unfurling of humanity's vast potential. It is an idea associated with all that is worldly and urbane, bringing nations together and standing against the primitive forces of tribalism and parochialism. In these commonplace mystifications globalization is not a greedy corporate strategy but rather the enlightened calibration of humanity with all that is reasonable and good.

Another reason that makes it difficult to appreciate the self-serving corporate agenda that drives the new world economy is that a new "globalized" world now stands against everyone, even the supercorporations that have been leading the globalizing charge over the last three decades. Finance capital beams money around the world at breakneck speeds; local and regional economies have become more integrated into global markets; events in one part of the world's economy reverberate everywhere else; it is common to consume products that come from remote corners of the globe; and more and more people feel connected by virtue of the internet. Everyone experiences a global village "out there" that can no longer be ignored—a world that is "digital," "knowledge-based," "virtual" and "connected."[1] Politicians truly feel constrained by the pressures of worldwide policy standards, standards that are invariably falling. Labour leaders formulate demands with an eye to global wage rates and collapsing workplace standards. Business leaders often experience restricted decision-making power in the face of global markets.

And so it is easy to be confounded by the idea of globalization. Its raw truth is missed easily in a world of ever-changing practices and untempered rhetorical flourishes. The challenge is to release ourselves from these mystifying clutches. We must turn and squarely face globalization's Machiavellian core: the struggle around labour costs manifested as a drive-down-wages imperative. Globalization is driven by the desire to lower wages around the world. It is about making people desperate enough to take low-paying jobs where they barely earn enough to survive. It is about delivering devastating blows to established unions and their members in the North. It is about brutally crushing any attempts to organize workers in the South. It is about creating large pools of underemployed people so that wages will remain low. It is about ruthlessly attacking social programs that are seen to prop up minimum wages. It is about callously attacking the poor themselves for fear that they might pass on a rotten job. For the business world caught in a struggle with workers in the era of worldwide capitalism, globalization is a tooth and nail strategy to depress wages. It is helpful to remember that corporations do not globalize because their executives have a penchant for warmer weather or spicy food.

A reader could be admired for cynically requesting a distinction between capitalism in general and the era that has come to be known as globalization. Has the history of capitalism not revolved around the struggle over wages, and is it not littered with stories about below-subsistence wages, attacks on workers, union-busting and massive pools of unemployed workers? What makes "globalization" different from "capitalism"? Have we somehow left capitalism behind? To complicate these interrogations there is a collection of terms like "information economy" or "post-industrial society" or "post-capitalist society" hanging in the air, suggesting strongly that the world today is different from the "capitalism" of the nineteenth and early twentieth centuries. The evidence adduced to support this claim, however, is usually superficial. From the perspective of the rudimentary conflicts that lie at the heart of a world organized around private property and wage labour, the world has not changed in any essential way, as a Mexican auto worker, a "guest" labourer in Kuwait or a seasonal employee in Prince Edward Island would incline to remind us. Terms that suggest that there has been a fundamental break from the past overdraw the degree of change in the world around us and are better understood as part of the ideological smokescreen emanating from specialists and pundits. At a very basic level there really is no difference at all. Globalization does not have an internal mechanism that is different from the conventional dynamic of class struggle in any capitalist society, and the lengths that corporations and businesses go to in order to gain an upper hand over their workers also fail to reveal anything new.

But something has changed. The old rounds and familiar refrains of capitalism are being played to new rhythms. The term globalization does help to capture the evolving political twists of this longstanding struggle between capital and labour over the last three decades. Globalization is a helpful idea in that it refers to a specific period in the history of capitalism, a period when a class compromise forged in the middle of the twentieth century is being rolled back.[2] If a good chunk of the twentieth century can be seen as the era of a long compact between the Northern working class and their capitalist counterparts, then the last three decades can be understood in terms of the systematic undoing of this compromise. Capital has been shredding its unprecedented agreement with labour that guided Northern societies for much of the post-Second World War period. Indeed, this makes the term globalization a bit ironic. It creates the impression of something that is going on around the world, and the idea seems apt if we merely dwell on the worldly nature of our economy. However, at its core globalization is about disciplining the working class in the North, in part by end-running it in favour of cheaper labour in the South. The globalizing economy has been triggered by this struggle to weaken the Northern worker. In this essential manner globalization is global only in a superficial spatial sense, at least at the outset; in its first moment it unfolds as a sustained attack on working people in the North. The compact that involved real gains for the Northern working class—and the shelving of a more transformative political agenda—is being systematically dismantled. To understand globalization in Atlantic Canada it is helpful to outline the main features of this historic transition.

The Twentieth-Century Fordist Compact

In time, the effects of globalization will certainly play themselves out socially and politically. As a multifaceted accumulation strategy globalization is fraught with all sorts of tensions and contradictions. In the short term it is impossible to know how far the roll back will go, but over the long haul the effects of this new global order will push capitalism along and lay the foundations for its metamorphosis into something very different. A few of these tensions and contradictions are noteworthy. Globalization harms the working people—this much is very clear—yet it also establishes the basis for a generalized increase in worker consciousness and coordinated resistance. It initially pits workers around the world against each other, especially those in the North and the South, but it also establishes the foundations for a more inclusive and lasting internationalism among all workers. In part, at least, globalization rests upon the development of new communications and technological applications that displace workers and intensify their exploitation and, yet, make the coordination of worker resistance much easier and smoother in the future. Capital has constructed a world that draws upon the mythologies of capitalism so aggressively, mythologies that stand so feebly against the growing misery of our globalizing world, that it is hard to believe that these mystifying devices will not reach some point of exhaustion in the future, creating unparalleled social incredulity in exploited people around the world and thus laying the basis for a clearer transformative agenda. For capital itself, as it seizes its capacity to move around the world and take advantage of cheaper labour, it simultaneously establishes the basis for a generalized uniformity of labour and production standards that will render the mobility of capital futile or inconsequential in the future. In the end, globalization is about transnational capital proceeding in a privileged and autocratic manner, and yet it lays down the conditions that will encourage its eventual eclipse and displacement. Capitalism is still sowing the seeds of its own demise—like a sun that becomes a "red giant" just before it burns itself out completely—although many left intellectuals have sadly lost touch with its destiny. Globalization is, in this sense, capitalism's "last hurrah."

All of this, however, is, as one might say, "down the road." Here the goal is to recognize that globalization emerged out of the disintegration of the post-Second World War compromise between capital and labour. The compromise was hammered out after decades of experimentation on the shop floor, innumerable economic upturns and downturns and periods of intense labour strife. We can begin to elaborate on the post-Second World War order and the eventual transition to globalization by observing that by the early twentieth century the system of production was epitomized by the widespread application of "scientific" methods. Efficiency was fast becoming the cardinal operating principle of production, and the conventional wisdom was to crank out as much product as (in)humanly possible. In the words of Frederick Winslow Taylor, after whom the ideas of "scientific management" came to be known:

> We can see our forests vanishing, our water-powers going to waste, our soil being carried by floods into the sea; and the end of our coal and our iron is in sight. But our larger wastes of human

effort, which go on every day through such of our acts as are blundering, ill-directed, or inefficient, and which Mr. Roosevelt refers to as a lack of "national efficiency," are less visible, less tangible, and are but vaguely appreciated.... No one can be found who will deny that in the case of any single individual the greatest prosperity can exist only when that individual has reached his highest state of efficiency; that is, when he is turning out his largest daily output. (1998: iii, 2)

Greater efficiency created a troublesome problem for the owners of the factories. They needed to match their refined capacity to produce with the ability of people to buy products. Capital has often been faced with the problem of overproduction, and this problem was all the more likely with the widespread adoption of "scientific" production. The business world desperately needed to sell all of its products, and in the first half of the twentieth century this was accomplished through the cultivation of a society of mass consumers. Corporations aggressively set about convincing people that they needed such things as an electric iron, a car or a hair curler. Indeed, it has been argued that the television was recognized as a useful invention only after corporate executives realized that they could use it to sell products to gullible North Americans and Europeans.[3] The consumer societies of the North had fully congealed by the post-Second World War period.[4]

Greater efficiency created another serious problem. Workers, especially artisans and skilled labourers, did not take kindly to "scientific" or Taylorist production techniques, mainly because they correctly understood that Taylorism would erode their skills and contribute to a general decline in their workplace power. Taylor himself (1998: 28) spoke of the difficulty of finding the "right" man for his time and motion experiments, and by "right" he meant submissive and thoughtless:

> Now one of the very first requirements for a man who is fit to handle pig iron as a regular occupation is that he shall be so stupid and so phlegmatic that he more nearly resembles in his mental make-up the ox than any other type. The man who is mentally alert and intelligent is for this very reason entirely unsuited to what would, for him, be the grinding monotony of work of this character.

The skilled labourer in the early twentieth century understandably resisted refinements to the labour process and played a significant role in the generalized resistance of workers, who often resorted to strikes, sit-ins and marches to improve their lot. In the end, worker restlessness throughout the early decades of the twentieth century contributed to rising real wages, and to a considerable extent this rise helped to pacify all workers. The corporate establishment grudgingly accepted the higher wages since it meant that people could consume more products. Indeed, many leaders of industry openly recognized this, and Henry Ford's famous $5 work-day—a strategy intentionally designed to allow Ford's workers to purchase his automobiles—captured this crude formula well. Companies that lacked Ford's social perspicacity fought tooth and nail with their workers over wage hikes, but unrelenting pressure from below continued to nudge the social wage upward.

Another boost for mass consumption would come with the growth of the Keynesian public policy framework. The longstanding concern over the boom and bust cycles of capitalism had sparked ongoing debates about how best to deal with them, with the goal being long-term profitability and economic stability. The idea of smoothing out capitalism's cyclical nature by means of state intervention was formalized in the writings of John Maynard Keynes. Keynes proposed that governments inject money into the economy during recessionary periods and remove a little money during periods of healthy growth, in effect managing the economy by managing the overall demand for goods and services. When the economy was slowing down, a little extra money could be put into people's pockets to sustain sundry consumption. And when the economy was heating up a little extra money could be taken out of their pockets to dampen consumption and stop the economy from overheating. It was recognized early that one of the easier ways to institutionalize "demand-side" management of the economy was through the state's social and infrastructural policies. Keynes's ideas, in effect, provided a sort of elite endorsement of working-class demands for better welfare policies, pension plans, unemployment insurance and so on. In the aftermath of the Second World War the welfare state expanded exponentially, and this growth was invariably justified in terms of Keynesian principles.

As shown in Figure 1.1 the two pillars of the twentieth-century compact include the mass production regime and the Keynesian public policy framework. The first pillar reflects the way corporations tended to organize themselves inside the factory, including the reluctant acceptance of a unionized and relatively well-paid work force. It embraces the idea of mass production for mass consumption. The second pillar reflects the general public policy principles that guided politicians throughout North America and Europe, and the spirit of these Keynesian principles embraces the idea of countercyclical state spending and is confirmed by the rise of the welfare state. Although analytically we can separate the two pillars of Fordism, it must be stressed that they formed part of a rudimentary compromise between capital and labour that had evolved over the decades covering the two world wars. The mass production regime grew directly out of conflicts inside the factories of the

Figure 1.1
Fordism (1945–1970)

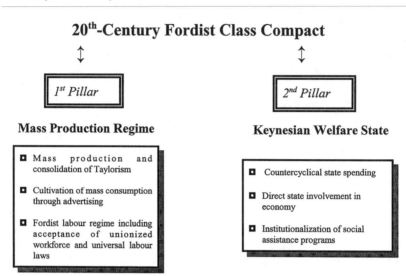

20ᵗʰ-Century Fordist Class Compact

1ˢᵗ Pillar

2ⁿᵈ Pillar

Mass Production Regime

Keynesian Welfare State

- Mass production and consolidation of Taylorism
- Cultivation of mass consumption through advertising
- Fordist labour regime including acceptance of unionized workforce and universal labour laws

- Countercyclical state spending
- Direct state involvement in economy
- Institutionalization of social assistance programs

North, especially the struggles to control production strategies on the shop floor and the battle for higher wages. Those struggles extended well beyond the factory gates. The Keynesian welfare state emerged out of the state's evolving mediation of class relations, and it absorbed working-class demands for social policies that shielded them from the harsher effects of capitalism, especially unemployment. This does not mean that during the Fordist era the working class gained all that it could, or even a lot for that matter, but simply that tentative resolutions to the tensions and antagonisms between the chieftains of capitalism and the working class were institutionalized and entrenched in the machinery of the state. The nexus of mass production for mass consumption and the Keynesian welfare state may have been formalized and championed by the apostles of economic thought during the heyday of Fordism, but their creation and consolidation were forged in struggle and infused with a sense of political sacrifice. They were factory-centred practices and public policy frameworks that temporarily resolved decades of grinding social conflict.

It is in this living and breathing way that the mass production conventions and the Keynesian public policy framework formed the two pillars of the historic compact between capital and labour. The compact was, first and foremost, a political covenant that institutionalized the temporary resolution of a class struggle that would continually evolve and change. Capital reluctantly granted concessions to labour to preserve the integrity of the system and to insure healthy investment returns; labour achieved real gains for working people throughout the North but stopped well short of challenging the general system of class exploitation. Capital was never terribly enthusiastic about its covenant with labour. In retrospect it seemed willing to cope with the Fordist compact only if the high levels of post-war profitability could be sustained.

The Eclipse of Fordism and the Rise of Globalization

In approaching our discussion of globalization in Atlantic Canada it is helpful to emphasize that the balance that had been struck between capital and labour was a gossamer. Indeed, less than three decades after the end of the Second World War events transpired that threw this historically tenuous compromise into relief. For two decades after the Second World War corporations around the world enjoyed unprecedented rates of profitability. Returns on investments often approached 15 percent in many economic sectors. As the 1960s progressed declines in the rate of profitability began to appear regularly throughout the North.[5] All economic sectors were hit hard, and although Japan was spared the first wave of falling profitability, by the early 1970s it had reached there also. The declines were steep and alarming. Rates of profit fell to less than 5 percent, and profitability rates of 2 or 3 percent were suddenly not uncommon in many sectors of the economy. By the early 1970s capital began to search in earnest for ways to restore its post-war rates of profitability, and these efforts would lead it to confront directly the Fordist arrangements.

As the 1970s wore on the Fordist nexus of mass production for mass consumption and the Keynesian policy framework fell under sustained scrutiny. A series of political developments, including the unilateral dismantling of the Bretton Woods system of fixed exchange rates by the United States along with the appearance of stagflation—high unemployment combined with high inflation—helped to encourage vocal critiques of both pillars of the historic understanding between capital and labour. On the side of the Fordist production customs, managerial criticism of the mass production reflex began to appear with greater regularity. A sense emerged that the staid modes of shop-floor organization in Europe and North America were weak in comparison with innovative approaches in Japan. There arose a willingness to experiment with alternative forms of production both inside and outside the factory. A greater sensitivity to the segmented and irregular nature of markets was also being refined in many corporate sectors, especially textiles. And with chronically high inflation, repeated calls by the corporate sector and politicians for wage "moderation" could be heard. Wage controls were eventually applied in a number of countries, and aggressive critiques of organized labour resurfaced with a new vigour. The mass production regime and much of its complementary labour regime were beginning to unravel.

The Keynesian policy framework also fell into public disrepute. The appearance of stagflation was altogether inconsistent with the premises of Keynesianism, suggesting as it did that the economy needed stimulation and sedation at the same time. State spending received special attention, and it became popular to claim that "excessive" spending aggravated inflation without necessarily reducing unemployment. By the mid-1980s the once unassailable idea that the state should intervene to manage the economy had lost most of its credibility. In the Canadian context, for example, the New Democratic government in Ontario tried to spend its way out of the recession of the early 1990s, only to encounter an explosion of public criticism animated by the demise of the Keynesian imprimatur. Critiques of countercyclical state intervention came to form the thin edge of the wedge as all state activity in the economy fell under sustained ideological assault by right-of-centre politicians, corporate lobbies and their media impresarios during the 1980s.

The decaying pillars of the twentieth-century compact reflected a strategy to restore earlier levels of profitability on the part of transnational capital. The appearance of the Trilateral Commission, comprised of representatives from the upper crust of North America, Europe and Japan, revealed the extent of the efforts afoot to forge an elite consensus on the post-Fordist world. In Canada, the formation of the Business Council on National Issues—a corporate lobby group drawn from 150 of the leading corporations in the Canadian economy—signalled the gestation of a new policy framework that would be more or less entrenched by the mid-1980s.

However, the glamourous convergence of power and wealth at the top must not distract our attention from their real task. We need to bear in mind that the representatives of transnational capital set about to do what any good business executive will do when confronted with profitability crises: reduce production costs, especially by reducing labour costs. When seen from this vantage point, the rise of globalization is not a mysterious development, although it is certainly cloaked in more than its fair share of hyperbole. The template of the new global economic and social order is informed by the drive to depress wages and significantly weaken labour. Of course, one could quickly learn that globalization is about many other things if all of its decision-making nooks and crannies were explored. Transnational capital will globalize to take advantage of new markets. Many companies are in the habit now of working out agreements to relocate production sites in certain countries, especially China, in exchange for market access. At other times they will globalize to allow for higher levels of intra-firm trading to reduce corporate taxes. The distribution of corporate facilities around the world allows corporations to control profit levels in any particular jurisdiction, which effectively allows them to rachet down local taxes. On still other occasions transnational capital will globalize to dodge tough environmental restrictions, re-establishing operations in areas where laws are less encumbering.

The efforts to cut into new markets, lower corporate taxes or take advantage of lax environmental restrictions, though, do not drive globalization. They are ancillary to the globalization agenda and merely constitute some of the auxiliary strategies pursued by brainy executives to maximize profits. They are good business practices in that they round out a multipronged effort to enhance the bottom line, but they do not make globalization happen. The *dynamos* of the historic transition, the logical kernel that accounts for the frazzling of Fordism and the rise of globalization is the struggle to lower labour costs.

Two broad strategies on the part of big business can be detected. The first involves a direct reorganization of corporate practices. To this end, transnational capital has reorganized production on the shop-floor, restructured corporations, offloaded and downloaded much of its production and reconfigured its labour force. The second strategy is the consolidation of a policy framework that emphasizes free markets and the autocracy of capital. Over time, and in view of its purported return to the principles of classical liberal political economy, this policy agenda has come to be known as neoliberalism.[6] To the overall series of non-Fordist production strategies adopted by capital since 1970 we can affix the term "globalization." And to the simultaneous development of a post-Keynesian policy framework aimed at undercutting working people the world over we also can affix the term "globalization." It is helpful to outline both of these strategies briefly.

The Restructuring of Capital

The restructuring of capital proceeds in two complementary directions, or modes. The first targets workers directly employed within the firm. The second expands the web of production to include workers outside the principal corporation, essentially farming out the conflict between management and workers to subordinate firms. Each mode aims to lower labour costs, and together they make up what tends to be called "flexible production."[7] Turning to the first mode, workers within the employ of principal corporations have experienced a reorganization of the shop-floor. The appearance of "lean production" methods, especially in the automobile industry, epitomizes these trends. These methods reflect three decades of workplace experimentation and job redesign that centre around the concepts of teamwork, job rotation, worker-based quality control and an overall emphasis on productive flexibility. Although these management philosophies are heralded as positive developments that have given workers more control over the workplace, in the end they deepen worker exploitation in an era of growing vulnerability and fear and do very little to alleviate the drudgery and tedium of most jobs.[8]

A more visible strategy is the wholesale relocation of corporate operations from Northern regions to Southern regions where labour laws are weaker or poorly enforced. More than two hundred zones of intensified production, sometimes called export processing zones (EPZs), have appeared around the world. The relocation of innumerable firms in the EPZs undergirds the rise of the so-called newly industrialized countries (NICs) in the South and extensive deindustrialization throughout the North. The term "rust-belt," referring as it does to this trend toward increasingly idle factories throughout Canada and the United States, has entered our popular lexicon. Corporate relocation is so common today that the notion of nationally based firms, signified by the term "multinational corporations," has given way to the concept of "transnational corporations," entities that are truly anchorless, bound by little and beholden to few.

The resettlement of transnationals to low-wage areas of the world provides the most dramatic example of corporate restructuring. When this happens the typical Fordist worker in the North—unionized, well paid, covered by decent benefits and so on—can be let go in favour of non-unionized, poorly paid workers in the South. These North/South wage differentials can be steep, ranging from $20 U.S. or more *per hour* in the North to less than a few dollars U.S. *per day* in the South. Wages of workers in the South, especially in the EPZs, usually fail to cover most basic needs. The disciplinary effect—wage discipline for the most part—that this corporate strategy has on labour in the North has been well documented. The widespread closure of operations by transnational firms throws fear into the hearts of those workers who remain employed. Union leaders are routinely threatened with further plant closures and are constantly reminded that they must be "flexible" during contract talks. This exacerbates the common tension between union leaders and the rank and file. Although bargaining committees commonly resort to wage and workplace concessions to avoid plant closures and minimize further job losses, the rank and file is often frustrated by these recommendations, and this increases stress within many unions whose ranks have already been depleted in the era of globalization. Everything augurs poorly for union growth and strengthening. In the North, workers fear that unionization will provoke plant closures and job losses. In the South unions can be kept out using much harsher tactics, including police repression and threats of dismissal, physical injury and, in some cases, murder.

For workers everywhere the capacity of large firms, especially transnational corporations, to pull up stakes and relocate elsewhere has meant lower across-the-board wage levels. The disciplinary effects of this capacity to move from place to place, however, go even further. Politicians recognize that tougher investment rules and regulations might force established companies to limit new investments or to leave altogether, which urges governments to create more attractive business climates. It could be said that a sort of "mobility logic" bears down on everyone or at least is believed by almost everyone, including many labour leaders who routinely sacrifice important goals of the labour movement to save jobs. Politicians seem bound by a higher order in the era of the new global economy. They stress that they must respond pragmatically to the new realities of globalization and regularly claim powerlessness in the face of global money markets that will not hesitate to inflict punitive runs on a country's currency. Moreover, they repeatedly remind the electorate about the importance of remaining competitive globally—which certainly legitimizes any efforts to repress demands for higher wages from working people. Corporate capital has used this vulnerability to chisel away at a wide range of policy options and, in the end, has passed off its self-serving agenda as the only viable alternative to economic and social chaos in the era of globalization. As Linda McQuaig (1998: 28) puts it:

> In the global economy, there is only one valid position, and it is the position traditionally known as "right-wing." But now it's been stripped of that "right-wing" label.... This position is now simply called "pragmatic," "realistic," in line with the "realities" of the global marketplace. What used to be seen as "right-wing" is now simply the reality. Policies that used to be clearly understood to favour the rich—policies that the rich have been pushing aggressively since time immemorial—are now presented as pragmatic and in everyone's interests.

Getting more out of its work force for less money is a defining feature of transnational capital in the era of globalization. But it has not stopped there. Countless firms have offloaded their labour conflicts through the combined use of short-term contracting (supply contracts renegotiated every few weeks or months); subcontracting (enlisting the services of outside companies to manufacture goods); outsourcing (enlisting firms to assemble products and to manufacture component parts); and contracting out (especially supportive services and special tasks). The practice of subcontracting stands out among corporate strategies that intentionally download labour problems to smaller firms. Nike Corporation, for example, does not own one production facility. Nike and so many other leading corporations dole out the manufacture of their products to secondary facilities around the world. These firms must then recruit and manage local workers drawn from the masses of poor and desperate citizens. The threat of losing future contracts with the parent corporation is enough to persuade the local entrepreneurs to manage their work force aggressively—resorting to ferocious anti-unionism, firings, threats and harassment—to maintain poor wages and working conditions and to avoid production interruptions. When workers do make meaningful advances against their local employers by modestly improving their wages or bettering their working conditions, the subcontracts are not as lucrative for the local elites. And, in a typical scenario, as standards for working people rose in South Korea and Taiwan, leading transnationals moved their contracts from those countries to Indonesia and Thailand during the 1980s and to Vietnam in the latter part of the 1990s (which, by the way, is the subtext to the thawing of U.S.–Vietnamese relations).

Transnational corporations are emerging as researchers and product designers, production coordinators and product marketers rather than direct manufacturers of products, a development that heightens the importance of patent laws and intellectual property rights. The strategy is simple but ingenious. Larger firms end run inevitable and intractable labour disputes by delegating much of their production and day-to-day operations to smaller firms spread around the globe. Throughout the South there is never a shortage of small-time capitalists, usually from leading local families with ignoble exploitative histories, who are more than willing to run the network of subfirms that makes shoes, apparel, toys, housewares and so on. This broader network of firms then confronts a labour force that is equally diffused and therefore considerably weakened. The advantage goes to capital, especially when the unqualified support of the state and its policing apparatus is taken into consideration. For transnational corporations working people do a sort of disappearing act; more to the point, by farming out much of the production the *dons* of capital charge small-time *capitaliosos* with the responsibility of "whacking" local workers.

The restructuring of capital can be summarized in terms of the notion of flexibility. One part of this is the gravitation toward more flexible production systems; the other involves the emergence of the flexible worker. Regarding the development of flexible production, it has been widely observed that firms are better able to retool quickly, to run small batches of goods, to accent products in the face of more open-ended consumer preferences and to coordinate production schedules with continually evolving markets. Capital's reforms have allowed it, in effect, to coddle global markets that it now recognizes as being segmented, unpredictable and capricious. This heightened responsiveness of production to fickle markets is manifested in the increased use of "small batch" production runs and "just-in-time" production; firms take the last-minute temperature of particular markets and adjust goods and output accordingly. The Fordist premise of mass production for mass consumption has partly given way to more flexible production for segmented consumption throughout many industries and within many firms.

The restructuring of production, however, was inconsistent with the

Fordist labour regime, which was widely regarded as uncooperative and uncompetitive—that is, inflexible with respect to wages. A labour force with elevated expectations about wage levels, the length and availability of employment, the nature of workplace conditions and the obligations of society was inconsistent with the transition to flexible production strategies. The cultural ideal of a worker in the Fordist era—one who is reasonably well paid; a member of a union as well as an employee of a firm; willing to work at tedious jobs for long hours in return for stable, long-term employment; protected by an array of laws governing labour relations and workplace conditions; and confident that the labour market or state social assistance would prevent one from personal misfortune and financial ruin—has been slowly giving way to the globalization era's cultural ideal of the "flexiworker"—a motivated member of the corporate team who is willing to move from job to job in lieu of long-term employment, to work irregular hours, to train and retrain endlessly for the "new economy," and to piece together a living on modest wages without expecting too much in the way of handouts from the state. Such a "flexiworker" is well suited to the new flexible production strategies, which include extensive corporate relocation to the South and consumer-friendly manufacturing strategies in the North. Indeed, as capital has quickly recognized, concerted efforts to match production with segmented markets requires a special type of worker—one who is flexible, simply grateful for employment from time to time and, above all, as cheap as possible.[9] Fordist workers with their characteristic expectations about working life and wages have been quickly regarded as anachronous in a world of plant closures, chronic unemployment, falling real wages and expanding part-time work.

It should be observed that many workers are more or less exempt from this aggressive push for a more flexible labour force. At its most general level globalization has continued to carve out a two-tiered work force around the world. The upper tier of core workers typically have university degrees, often more than one, in law, engineering, accountancy, business, administration and the natural sciences. These core workers are concentrated in the North, although a bevy of skilled professionals will always accompany a firm anywhere in the world. They undertake a number of critical tasks including product research and design, production design, management operations, marketing, accounting, legal work and public relations. These core workers tend to fetch the higher salaries within the corporate structure, and their jobs tend to be more secure than their counterparts at the second tier of global production. These professionals, however, are quite distinct from the upper-echelon executives, who make most corporate decisions and who are probably best understood as delegates of the families of capital.

The core workers contrast sharply with the massive body of peripheral workers at the lower tier. Whereas the core workers are likely to think of themselves as being on career paths, the peripheral workers are more likely to think of themselves as merely having jobs—typically tiresome, tedious jobs that often fail to cover the basic necessities of life. The peripheral workers can be found anywhere in the world, although their relative numbers have been increasing in the South. The sobering litany of abuse of workers around the world is inflicted on the peripheral work force, whose members are seen by capital as expendable. The Fordist era's "noble toiler" largely has been displaced by peripheral workers with the right "attitude" for jobs that are anything but fulfilling and rewarding— workers ensconced in factories, offices, mines, restaurants, stores and so forth. A movement has been afoot to acclimatize working people to the idea that a full-time, life-long job with respectable wages and decent benefits is increasingly passé. The unmistakable tendency is toward short-term positions, often with part-time hours, iffy wages and few benefits.

The effort to create a "new worker" suitable to the renovated profit-seeking strategies of corporate capital is not the end of the restructuring story. To expose the Northern worker completely, capital has had to get to its institutional supports reflected in the Keynesian welfare state. In other words, the transition to globalization has not unfolded entirely within the factory. It is to this second half of the globalization agenda that we now turn.

The Neoliberal Policy Framework

To roll back the historic compromise capital could make only so much progress in the world of business. To finish the job it needed to focus on government to undercut the Keynesian policy framework that had served Northern governments and provided meaningful protections and safe-guards for Northern workers since the end of the Second World War. Much of the Fordist compact had become institutionalized in public policies and laws ranging from income supports and social assistance programs to reasonably strong labour codes. From the vantage point of big business the institutionalization of the Keynesian welfare state would have to be scaled back as part of the generalized attack on wages and working people. By the late 1970s the public disavowal of Keynesianism and everything that went with it made it abundantly evident that the world had entered the twilight of the post-Second World War compro-mise. Transnational capital was earnestly promoting a revamped policy framework better suited to its globalizing agenda, especially its increased tendency to exploit pools of cheap Southern labour.

This post-Keynesian policy framework is conventionally known as neoliberalism.[10] As the term suggests, the emphasis is on a return to liberal economic ideals of the past, particularly regarding free markets. Contemporary commentators tend to place an unqualified emphasis on free market solutions for most of society's problems. The basic policy refrain is unmistakable: If it's broken, then expose it to the free market; and if it isn't broken, make it look broke and draw it into the free market fold anyway. The free market is championed as possessing a natural corrective mechanism capable of bringing the greatest good to the greatest number of people. The political corollary of this vaguely utilitarian commitment to free markets is the rejection of state activity in the economy. The Keynesian ideas that ratified government intervention throughout the early post-Second World War period have been replaced by the conviction that the state, as a rule, has little or no place in the economy, except to guarantee the operation of free markets. Neoliberal devotees believe that when the state intervenes it distorts natural market forces and creates waste and inefficiency, in part because bureaucrats and other state functionaries lack the necessary incentive to be frugal. It can be said that neoliberalism is anti-statist at its core. More to the political point, it is an ideological rejection of government—only insofar as its policies and programs are implicitly seen to prop up the social wage—dressed up in the language of classical liberal economic analysis and its purported celebration of free markets.

During the 1980s growing concern about state indebtedness around the world provided a boost for the neoliberal cause. The growth of public debt in the North was blamed on careless state spending by profligate politicians. Fiscal crises contributed to a culture of austerity in countries around the world as governments cut programs, slashed spending and abandoned policies once thought unassailable. According to the prevailing wisdom of the 1980s and '90s, states running steep yearly deficits and accumulating massive public debts would have to stop spending their way out of economic and social problems and begin lowering deficits by reigning in public spending and scaling back the state. Hence, the solution to the problem of rising debt was virtually indistinguishable from those policies that promoted "free marketism." Both admonished politicians to downsize the state. Neoliberal followers were, in a sense, blessed with high public debt. They called for less government, and they took advantage of the high public debt to gain priceless credibility for their demands to cut services, slash social programs, roll back the civil service, privatize public corporations and deregulate the economy.

The first basket of neoliberal policies directly encourages the expansion of free markets. Figuring most prominently here are policies that institutionalize open trade between countries and deny trade barriers as an appropriate way to order international economic relations. The gravitation towards more liberal trading regimes is epitomized by the North American Free Trade Agreement (NAFTA) and its likely successor the Free Trade Agreement of the Americas (FTAA). Another element in this basket of free market policies is the deregulation of economic sectors, including utilities, telecommunications and the airline industry. In the neoliberal era, states are also more likely to offload public corporations, as evidenced by the privatization drives that have swept through the North.

According to neoliberal defenders these policies encourage the undistorted operation of economic markets; free markets are the best way to promote economic efficiency and maximize growth. In point of fact, common corporate practices such as oligopolies and interlocking corporate directorships throw this ideological sham of the business world into relief. Corporate support for free markets is relatively weak and selective in practice, but to the extent that support of the principle of free markets helps to erode the institutions of the state and weaken worker protections the corporate world's support is resounding and unqualified. We must momentarily take notice of the fact that a free reign in its struggles against labour is not quite the same as a free market. Except for the boasts of ideologues, who are charged with the task of glorifying the free market, the corporate echelons have few illusions about the real effects of free-market evangelizing. The support for open trading regimes, for example, has less to do with free markets in any competitive sense than it does with gaining access to cheap labour and then establishing unrestricted intra-firm trading across borders so that the advantages of the cheap labour are not cancelled out by high tariffs.

Organized labour has been hammered by the free market ethos and, to defend itself in the short run, it has often been drawn into petty protectionist positions that further undermine international solidarity. Free marketism became virtually synonymous with the atmosphere of austerity and fear that descended upon the Northern worker in the 1980s and 1990s, contributing significantly to cheaper labour costs for large and small corporations alike.

The ideological veil of free marketism is complemented by a second basket of neoliberal policies aimed at undercutting and rolling back established social programs. These policies assume many different forms, including complete program cuts, program consolidation, program contractions, changes in eligibility requirements and reduction of benefits. The relationship of these changes to debt hysteria is straightforward: first, express concern about the debt; blame the debt on excessive social spending, irrespective of the facts; be sure to attack politicians for carelessly spending in the past; commit oneself to "responsible" spending and call it "getting your fiscal house in order"; and then promise to cut funding for social programs as the ultimate act of social and political responsibility. In the Northern industrialized countries twenty years of underfunding has done a lot of damage to countless social programs, while many others were cut completely. In the Canadian context, reforms to the Employment Insurance system, the tightening of eligibility requirements and decreases in social assistance rates in the aftermath of the federal government's cessation of the Canada Assistance Plan in 1995, as well as funding cuts in education, typify neoliberal policies routinely justified as being fiscally responsible. Indeed, chronic underfunding in education, health care and the provision of utilities such as electricity and water have heightened public anxiety and forced incremental privatization as those with the means explore alternatives such as bottled water or private pensions.

The social equation of neoliberal policy reforms is clear: social austerity equals low wages. The choking of social assistance programs and other reforms drive people into low-wage jobs with poor working conditions. Neoliberal social policies, to employ gentler language, help moderate the social wage. Even in the face of irregular hours, daycare challenges, sexual harassment from bosses, customer mistreatment and chronic workplace stress, workers are now more likely to calculate that it is better to persevere through a rotten job rather than face the crushing indignities of severely eroded social assistance rates. In this manner the culture of austerity forces otherwise reluctant workers into the labour market and thus helps to keep wages down. Restaurant owners, tourist operators, seasonal processing firms, retailers and so on are able to hold a hard line on wages knowing that deteriorating social assistance programs will force recalcitrant workers into the work force. Rather than reforming the terms of employment in a way that respects human dignity, therefore, neoliberal social reforms reduce the likelihood that a worker could hold out for better work by relying on state assistance. As every worker knows all too well, the money for rent and food has to come from somewhere, and, if declining rates of social assistance fail to cover the basic necessities of life, then one must take any job that comes along. Neoliberalism brings the threat of misery that capitalism holds over the heads of all workers one step closer to reality for those sitting on the margins of the labour force.

The third basket of neoliberal policies targets working people directly. These include a sustained decline in the real minimum wage, the weakening of enforcement mechanisms for labour laws, the stagnation in labour codes and regulations, the erosion of universal legal protections by permitting shop-floor agreements to override existing labour standards, and a greater tendency to resort to back-to-work legislation and to broaden the definition of "essential service." These practices have been accompanied by a protracted public condemnation of unionized workers throughout the North for their supposed "inflexibility" in the face of increased global competition. Many organized workers, especially public sector workers, have faced a kind of "worker bashing" akin to the bashing of poor people that figures so prominently in the neoliberal agenda. The consequences of these policies has been the further weakening of organized labour, which is already struggling to keep up with the consequences of extensive corporate restructuring. Unions harmed by declining memberships in the era of globalization now face a tougher time protecting workers from falling wages, employment insecurity and deteriorating workplace conditions. Non-unionized workers are as vulnerable as ever and often find it more difficult to organize and thereby resist the predations of their employers. Neoliberalism has dealt all workers a harsh blow, and the stagnation and decline in traditional legal protections round out a generalized assault that leaves workers scrambling to shield themselves from increasingly brazen business practices, corroded government programs and the unpredictability of the job market.

The Fate of Atlantic Canadians in the Era of Globalization

Globalization demonstrates poignantly that the nationally based labour compacts of the twentieth century were handicapped when capital decided to internationalize aggressively.[11] But capital's advantage is a short-term one. It can roll back regional class compacts by virtue of its capacity to globalize, but labour will eventually and inevitably "catch up" with capital and begin to rachet up labour standards once again. A renewed worker internationalism will inevitably follow this phase of globalization. These immanent historical tendencies cannot be sidestepped by anyone, least of all by the families of capital. For all of the ideological mystifications associated with globalization—mystifications that have done their part to distort labour's response to the globalization push over the last three decades—it is worth bearing in mind that unbelievably vast quantities of brutish repression and coercion have already been necessary throughout the South to stop labour from driving up workplace standards and wages. And when this finally happens, when the roll-backs of globalization have been reversed and then some, new crises will emerge that will inevitably shake the system to its very foundation. There will be no place left for capital to run.

Once again, we are a little ahead of ourselves. Figure 1.2 reviews the transition from Fordism to globalization. Most countries have gravitated toward the globalization regime in the face of intense international pressure. The Washington Consensus,[12] as the agenda of the new international economic order is frequently termed, is constructed around liberalized trading order and corporate-friendly national policies. This framework, moreover, is embedded within pivotal institutions such as the International Monetary Fund (IMF), the World Bank and the World Trade Organization (WTO). These bodies tirelessly promote the unfettered operation of corporations around the world. The WTO in particular, a relatively young organization that emerged out of the General Agreement on Tariffs and Trade regime (the GATT), has been playing a leading role in the creation of more liberal trading and investment regimes as it acquires the de facto authority to set international trading and investment rules and to

Figure 1.2
Globalization (early 1970s to present)

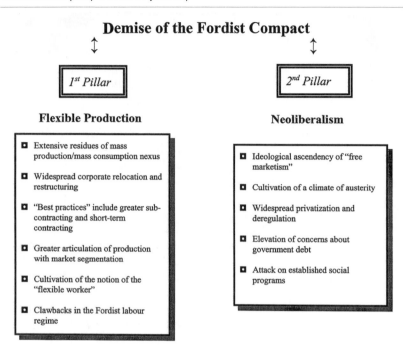

Demise of the Fordist Compact

| 1st Pillar | 2nd Pillar |

Flexible Production

- Extensive residues of mass production/mass consumption nexus
- Widespread corporate relocation and restructuring
- "Best practices" include greater sub-contracting and short-term contracting
- Greater articulation of production with market segmentation
- Cultivation of the notion of the "flexible worker"
- Clawbacks in the Fordist labour regime

Neoliberalism

- Ideological ascendency of "free marketism"
- Cultivation of a climate of austerity
- Widespread privatization and deregulation
- Elevation of concerns about government debt
- Attack on established social programs

censure any state that fails to comply with those standards. The IMF is also playing a leading role in the promotion of the Washington Consensus. Its activities range from studies on national economies to the provision of credit lines for governments facing currency or fiscal crises. In circumstances where a national government requires infusions of cash to stabilize its currency, for example, the IMF imposes "conditionality" on the recipient state by refusing to grant loans unless it adjusts its government policies in accordance with neoliberal ideals. More specifically, the IMF requires recipient national governments to adopt policies that scale back state involvement in the economy, roll back social programs and relax laws that hinder or restrict investment in any way. The economically troubled state is required to "structurally adjust" its national policy framework in accordance with the Washington Consensus.

In the North, the consolidation of the Washington Consensus has involved the much more direct influence of transnational capital, creating a sort of voluntary structural adjustment akin to the neoliberal measures imposed by the IMF on economically troubled nations. In Canada, for example, the political agenda of the last two decades—debt reduction, tax reform, free trade, deregulation and so forth—has been pushed and refined by the Business Council on National Issues (BCNI).[13] Other corporate-sponsored organizations complement the BCNI, including the C.D. Howe Institute in Toronto, the Fraser Institute in Vancouver and the Atlantic Institute for Market Studies in Halifax. Direct transmission lines between the representative organizations of transnational capital and the state have expanded. Indeed, the BCNI has become so dominant in Canada that serious concerns have arisen regarding the sovereignty of the Canadian state and the erosion of Canadian "democracy." Murray Dobbin reveals the depth of this concern for some commentators:

> As Canadians approach the millennium we find ourselves in a world dominated at every turn by large corporations.... Corporate domination, brazen, ruthless, ever more powerful, is evident everywhere as civilization seems to devolve in its path. The values of what we normally understand as civilization are swept aside by the new corporate imperative and its accompanying ideology. Thousands of years of human development and progress are reduced to the pursuit of "efficiency," our collective will is declared meaningless compared to the values of the marketplace, and communitarian values are rejected in favour of the survival of the fittest. A thinly disguised barbarism now passes for, is in fact promoted as, a global human objective. It is not only the best we can expect; it is the goal we should be seeking. (1998: 1–2)

This study refuses to refract the intensified class war waged on working people in the region with courtly discussions about the erosion of democracy or any of the other "comfort thoughts" of the intelligentsia. The Canadian state has been "democratic" only in the most vulgar of senses. And, regardless of the level of "democracy" that aptly characterizes it, it is being undermined as part of the generalized attack on working people. Since so much of the historic covenant between the classes was embedded in the institutions of the state, it should come as no surprise that any attempt to change the covenant would be pressed through its institutions. Notwithstanding the reactionary claim of Samuel Huntington and the Trilateral Commission[14] that the West suffers from an "excess of democracy," transnational capital could just as easily support the expansion and strengthening of many of the democratic institutions in Canada and elsewhere if that served its purpose (as the BCNI hints at when it reasserts its faith in parliamentary democracy in the face of street-level protests against globalization). Capital is not antidemocratic; it is antiworker. If throwing a democratic bone or two to "citizens" would do it any good, transnational capital would embrace any element of democracy in an instant. Discussions that centre around the notion of "democracy" are likely to miss the crucial and most important point about the evolving globalist agenda, namely, that the purportedly democratic institutions of the state are being attacked and usurped to undermine the relative power of working people. Almost invariably, these overworked dramatizations about the erosion of democracy give themselves over to genteel concerns about the importance of salvaging great nations such as Canada.[15] Analysts must do more than chase the shadows of a world that emits such cruelty and suffering.

Globalization is alive and well in Atlantic Canada, but the story has little to do with the erosion of democracy. Voluntary structural adjustment and its antiworker consequences are amply evident in Newfoundland and Labrador, Nova Scotia, Prince Edward Island and New Brunswick. Provincial governments have enthusiastically embraced every aspect of the neoliberal agenda, and, as in the case of New Brunswick, have sometimes prided themselves for the leading role played within the Canadian federation. Throughout the 1990s, New Brunswick's Frank McKenna boasted that the province was "Canada's laboratory," willing to forge ahead experimentally with neoliberal policies while the rest of the country took notes. The neoliberal policy framework, including the rising concerns about public debt, the celebration of the free market, extensive restructuring to social assistance, stagnating minimum wages, the downsizing of government, the privatization of public firms, the weakening of labour laws and municipal restructuring, is front and centre in the contemporary policy landscape of the region.

The ascendency of the neoliberal agenda means that life will be getting considerably more difficult for many Atlantic Canadians. Globalization is not about improving the living standards of working people around the world. Indeed, its aims are exactly the opposite. Capital has felt for three long decades that the goal of restoring post-Second World War levels of profitability will be best achieved by driving down wages around the world, and globalization is an orchestrated strategy premised upon this basic goal. Since globalization is about driving down wages, it is also about making life more difficult for working people. Social standards are in decline everywhere. According to the logic of globalization, it is better that nations cling to the bottom rung of the social standards ladder rather than sway precariously from its top, and nary a politician has failed to learn this lesson. The race to the bottom—as it has been dubbed by many critics—is not an accident. David C. Korten's wry assessment of globalization captures this relationship well:

> In the world of big money ... greed is a worker who wants a living wage.... To the global economy, people are not only increasingly unnecessary, but they and their demands for a living wage are a major source of economic inefficiency. (1995: 231)

As the post-Fordist production regime and free-market policy framework congeal three aspects of the attack on working people in Atlantic Canada can be discerned, and each aspect is addressed here in its own chapter. The first aspect concerns the sustained assault on the classic Fordist worker, that is, unionized workers receiving respectable wages and benefits. Before globalization, the quintessential Fordist worker could be found in both private and public sectors across Europe and North America. From the perspective of transnational capital and, for that matter, all other factions of capital, the Fordist worker was shielded by too many laws and protected by unions that were far too powerful. With the onset of profitability crises at the end of the 1960s and into the 1970s the Fordist labour regime stood in the way of a quick fix. Labour costs had to be lowered and the corporate elite quickly concluded that the protected Northern worker was too inflexible and uncompetitive. During the same period, transnational capital became increasingly attuned to the fact that years of capitalist intensification across the South, especially in export agricultural industries, had created severe social dislocations and made large pools of displaced peasants available for work. The real possibility of weakening labour in the North presented itself as capital relocated to the low-wage zones in the South. This strategy has shaken the Fordist labour regime more than anything else. In one stroke, capital lowered wage costs and broke the back of the Northern worker. Labour unions in the North have been thrown on the defensive in the face of massive layoffs and dismissals. Union membership has declined, real wages have been stagnating or falling and labour laws have been rolled back. The Fordist labour regime has been wobbling for more than two decades. No worker has stood on the sidelines of this crisis. In Chapter 2 attention is turned to the sustained attack on the Fordist labour umbrella in the region, including the weakening of traditional unions, the stagnation in real wages and the weakening of labour legislation.

The second aspect of the attack on working people focuses on direct efforts among workers who were indirectly part of the Fordist labour regime. These workers tended to be in non-unionized, low-wage sectors but were still entitled to the protections offered by labour laws. To keep wages down the corporate trust has relentlessly attacked unionization drives in the rapidly expanding service sector, choked the minimum wage, undermined social income supports and been indifferent to chronic unemployment and underemployment. The combined effects of these tactics have expanded the numbers of the working poor throughout the North. For more and more people a job is no longer an antidote to poverty; the wages from long hours of work often fail to cover basic needs. The growth of the working poor is a disturbing fact of life in the era of globalization. Chapter 3 addresses their swelling ranks across Atlantic Canada.

The third manifestation of the attack on working people around the world is evident in the growth of poverty. Poverty is not an accident of globalization; it helps to insure that a pool of reserve workers is always ready to be activated and pressed into service. A mass of desperately impoverished people permits corporations to abuse workers by means of low wages and poor working conditions. Agitation against this abuse typically results in sacking, by the hundreds in some parts of the world. Capital is confident that the bank of reserve workers can easily replenish the workplace. In the absence of poverty, of course, wages and working conditions around the world would improve, as workers who resisted and agitated could no longer be dismissed with impunity. To state it bluntly, globalization is about finessing a necessary baseline of poverty. Although the loyalists of globalization regularly remind the world that its prosperity will "trickle down" to all, the simultaneous expansion of the poor and indigent on one side and the super-rich on the other reveals the flimsy nature of their claims. From the vantage point of global capital poverty is a good thing; it enhances the prospects for healthy profits. Throughout the North poverty assures that there will be a pool of workers available for low-end jobs, especially in the rapidly expanding service sector. Throughout the South poverty is the whip that forces unwilling workers into the "dark Satanic mills"[16] of the early twenty-first century. Well-meaning politicians who fail to grasp this rudimentary link and who campaign on behalf of the poor are quickly disciplined by the corporate order or are marginalized altogether if their protestations persist. Poverty is a fact of life in Atlantic Canada. Chapter 4 examines its persistence in greater detail, especially regarding the relationship between poverty and low-wage work.

In Chapter 5 we look at the political side of globalization across the region. The politics of globalization are rich and replete with inescapable tensions and contradictions. The affairs of small firms and medium-sized businesses, for example, occasionally run up against the preferences of mammoth transnational corporations. Nevertheless, the free-market mantra prevails in every corner of the globe and invariably echoes in the mainstream media. In Atlantic Canada and elsewhere this free-market discourse draws upon an assortment of groundless beliefs, baseless claims and empty mythologies to win over its victims—at least in the short run. Although it services a rather narrow stratum of the world's population, free marketism is cloaked in a litany of discursive stratagems; repeated public claims; familiar turns of phrase; outright threats; fearmongering; the promotion of generalized anxiety; political pandering; the encouragement of racial and ethnic hatreds; the demonization of critics; and vocal attacks upon victimized social groups, especially women and the poor. Chapter Five surveys many of these rhetorical techniques as they are deployed by regional politicians. Regardless of its ring of familiarity, this public side of globalization amounts to a new demagoguery with a clear political and social agenda: enhance the conditions of corporate profitability. Anything goes everywhere if it has to. If globalization means militarizing an illegitimate regime in Columbia, forcing Jordanian peasants to pay through the nose for bread, uprooting the people of the Niger River delta, outlawing trade unions in Malaysia or, to bring the discussion back to the region, lecturing to a laid-off miner in Sydney about the virtues of retraining for the "new economy," then these are rationalized by intellectuals and trivialized by politicians as the price to be paid for progress. It should be stressed at the outset, however, that there are no conniving villains secretly formulating plans to methodically dupe the world's people. The fustian fields of globalization are a complex growth of self-serving corporate rationalizations, think-tank reports, media forays, university productions, political spindoctoring and, at times most importantly, the cunning of mediocrity.[17] Free marketism is the received sophistry of the age.

Of course, there is another side to the politics of the new world economy. The hegemonic story of globalization as narrated by elites runs headlong into the real experiences of working people around the world. Its falsehoods, exaggerations and inflated claims do not settle easily upon the minds of those on the receiving end of globalization's mounting exploitation. Its velvety rhetoric collides abruptly with the growing hardship and privation among so many of the world's people. All the hyperbole in the world cannot erase the experiences and cumulative wisdom of those who endure life in a shanty town, who struggle inside the modern high-tech sweatshops, who face years of irregular employment, who anxiously sweat it out in a local unemployment office or who suffer through the condescension of a welfare officer. A different sense of globalization is emerging from the ground up, and these countervailing understandings are translating into direct action against the globalization agenda. Considerable coercion from local authorities is necessary to keep this opposition in check. As globalization congeals institutionally the world witnesses the coalescence of naysayers in Seattle, Washington, Prague, Davos and Quebec City, to say nothing of the invisible acts of defiance by indomitable workers who will often risk all to organize their fellow employees, who demonstrate in remote villages, who resist the sexual predations of managers or who, even more poignantly perhaps, simply walk away from their jobs in the absence of any employment alternatives. The harmful effects of globalization have fostered a plethora of opposition groups and coalitions. These political forces strive to undo the harmful effects of the new world economy and, in some cases, to reverse the process of globalization altogether. Atlantic Canada has seen its share of political resistance in the era of globalization and in Chapter 5 we explore some of these struggles.

Notes

1. For a discussion of these themes and some of the analytical problems they highlight see Ursula Huws 1999.
2. A similar periodization and characterization of recent history appears in Laxer 1999. The distinction here, however, is perfectly consistent with efforts to periodize imperialism, and shares the spirit of Petras and Veltmeyer 2001.
3. One of the earlier versions of this argument can be seen in Mander 1978.
4. In the present era, of course, businesses spend much more time convincing people to purchase their particular brands, working from the premise that people believe they need most items. Only the quantity of disposable income tends to stand in the way of consumption.
5. This study is informed by the basic Marxist idea about the falling rate of profitibility in capitalism and is less persuaded by recent efforts to rework this elementary insight in the monopoly capitalist school. For an example of an argument centred around the falling rate of profit see Duménil et al. 1985. For a review of efforts to rework this basic position see Foster 2000.
6. It should be stressed that classical liberal political economy never blindly espoused the idea that the free market could solve most of the problems in society. Although there are clear links between neoliberalism and classical political economy, it would be wrong to assume that the latter tradition maintained such a vulgar attitude towards the state and its function in capitalist societies. See John Stuart Mill 1994, especially Book V, *Principles of Political Economy* (Oxford: Oxford University Press, 1994).
7. The transition to flexible production has received much attention. For an example of this literature see Smith 1994 or Fox and Sugiman 1999.
8. For a critical review of many of these workplace trends see James Rinehart 1998.
9. For a treatment of some elements of this idea see Gray 1998. For an exploration of some of these ideas in the Canadian context see Swift 1995.
10. One of the best reviews of neoliberalism may be found in Teeple 2000.
11. Discussions about class politics are rich and wide ranging at this moment. For example, see Danford 1997.
12. The Washington Consensus reflects the favoured basket of neoliberal policies and corporate practices emerging from the influence of U.S.-centred transnational interests. Its emphasis is on liberal trading regimes and minimal government interference in the so-called "free market." It is sometimes contrasted with a slightly different and very secondary package of neoliberal policies emerging out of the Pacific region and centred in Tokyo.
13. Although the rise of globalization can be addressed in terms of the supposed erosion of democracy throughout the North, these discussions rapidly lose sight of the fact that working people are the targets of the supercorporate agenda. The struggle between classes in Canada is not completely reflected in the evolution—democratic or otherwise—of the Canadian state.
14. To explore the politics surrounding the construction of consensual Western practices in the post-Fordist era see Gill 1990.
15. Indeed, the notion of democracy often becomes a sort of shorthand for the petty-nationalist idea of "Canada" as we see in discussions emerging out of

the Council of Canadians. One cannot help but feel, at times at least, that the concern is about "Canada" first and foremost and about the assault on the working class only in a secondary sort of way.

16. A quotation from the poem "Milton" (1804–08) by English poet and artist William Blake (1757–1827).

17. Globalization provides some of the best examples of the Orwellian manipulation of things. It is worth noting that the politicians who legislate the global neoliberal agenda routinely fail the most rudimentary knowledge tests about history and society and demonstrate a stunning inability to carry an argument. For a discussion of the general decline of political debate and commentary in recent decades see Lasch 1995.

Chapter 2

Wither the Fordist Worker
in Atlantic Canada

We often hear good things about the economy in Atlantic Canada. A feature article published in the *Canadian Economic Observer* in December 2000 (Statistics Canada 2000) was full of praise for the region. It reported that all four provinces were experiencing strong economic growth, in part because of Hibernia and the Sable Offshore Energy Project. The report noted that the 6 percent growth in Newfoundland and Labrador's economy in 1999 "continued to outpace the national average" (Statistics Canada 2000: 3.4). It stressed that in the same year Nova Scotia's GDP increased by 5.2 percent and Prince Edward Island's GDP grew by 3.2 percent. It also reported that as the 1990s drew to a close the province of New Brunswick "enjoyed its best growth of the decade, rising 4.2 percent" (Statistics Canada 2000: 3.5). The per capita GDP in Newfoundland and Labrador, Prince Edward Island and New Brunswick posted growth rates above the Canadian average. Because of the strong performance of the Atlantic Canadian provinces during the 1990s the article emphasized that "the gap between richest and poorest provinces narrowed" (Statistics Canada 2000: 3.2). A press release by the Atlantic Provinces Economic Council (APEC) in the summer of 2000 delivered a similarly optimistic message about the regional economy. APEC claimed that during the latter part of the 1990s the region had experienced its strongest growth since the mid-1980s and that the improved economy "led to stronger income, employment and consumer spending in many parts of Atlantic Canada" (APEC 2000).

Not all the news about the economy in Atlantic Canada, however, was as upbeat. A study by Statistics Canada released in the winter of 2000 revealed that income inequalities in the four Atlantic Canadian provinces increased between 1980 and 1998 (Sanga 2000). The study employed a measure called the "income inequality ratio," a measure which compares the income for families in the upper-income quintile with the income of families in the lower-income quintile. To illustrate, if families in the upper quintile receive five dollars of income for every dollar of income going to families in the lowest quintile, then the income inequality ratio would be five. The study found that the income inequality ratio had risen in every Atlantic Canadian province during the 1980s and 1990s. For every dollar of market income going to families in the lowest quintile in 1980 in Nova Scotia, for example, families in the upper quintile received $11.80. By 1998 the income inequality ratio had ballooned to $19.20 in Nova Scotia, a rise in the income inequality ratio of $7.40. An even larger increase occurred in New Brunswick, where the ratio went from $13.10 in 1980 to $20.80 in 1998, a rise of $7.70. Nova Scotia and New Brunswick, the provinces with the greatest concentration of economic activity in Atlantic Canada, experienced an average increase in the income inequality ratio of $7.50 over the survey period. Similar concerns about growing inequality among Atlantic Canadians were voiced by Genuine Progress Index (GPI)-Atlantic, a non-partisan, non-profit research group established in the region in 1997. Using the province of Nova Scotia as a focal point for the development of its indicators, GPI-Atlantic aims to develop indices of sustainable development and well-being for Atlantic Canadians. In the summer of 2001, GPI-Atlantic released a sixty-page report on the distribution of income in Nova Scotia. Among its other findings, the study reported that 80 percent of Nova Scotians had become worse off during the 1980s and 1990s, despite the fact that the provincial economy had grown steadily (GPI-Atlantic 2001).

With the good news comes bad news. The economy of the region is doing relatively well, but it is clear that prosperity and the fruits of economic growth have not been shared evenly among Atlantic Canadians over the last two decades. Observers have been inexorably drawn towards the tired observation that the rich appear to be getting richer and the poor poorer. Such studies serve an important function. They help to deflate the claims made by politicians and business leaders that everyone benefits equally from globalization. They run counter to the cherished idea that the generation of wealth in the era of globalization necessarily "trickles down" to everyone, and they thereby encourage a second look at the economic wisdom that guides contemporary policy makers. When an institution as corporate-friendly as Statistics Canada reports that the benefits of globalization have been "trickling up" over the last two decades across Atlantic Canada, even the most hardened neoliberal apologist has some explaining to do.

Nevertheless, these critiques do not go far enough. Statistics about income distribution do not provide a clear picture of recent economic developments in Atlantic Canada. A transition from vague measures of income level to more specific accounts of the direct consequences of globalization for working people is required. Analysis has to get beyond stories about the rich and the poor and directly examine the working lives of people who are tied to the Atlantic Canadian economy in a variety of ways. Dividing Atlantic Canadians up according to the size of their bank accounts can only take us so far. Quite frankly, it is doubtful whether many of the neoliberal faithful really buy into the conventional economic wisdom about growing prosperity for all, and a little savvy could easily lead one to suspect that their claims are transparently self-serving. To avoid being critical in vain, our analysis must come to focus squarely on the changing character of working life, on the struggle over wages, on the collective capacities of workers and, more generally, on the ways in which countless employers and businesses have been able to extract much more out of Atlantic Canadians each day. The worsening picture of income distribution in the last two decades confirms many fears and cynical expectations, but a concerted analytical effort is still required to clarify the long-term effects of globalization on working people and the marginalized poor across the region. We must enlist an approach that allows us to peer into the working lives of working people, to acquire a better sense of their workplace trials and tribulations, and to explore the real human consequences of contemporary economic policy.

To make this necessary transition it is helpful to reflect on one of globalization's many ironies. Some accounts suggest that what is exceptional about globalization is its destruction of anything truly exceptional, its ceaseless attack on alternative ways of living and its unrelenting standardization of life. It might be said that what is remarkable about globalization is its capacity to erode anything genuinely remarkable, its levelling of the world into what is sometimes called McWorld. When reflecting on this irony, globalization does not appear very global in any cosmopolitan or culturally inclusive sense of the word. Rather, it appears as the seemingly inexorable advance of one vision of life, the Western capitalist way of life as carried along by the policy preferences of very big corporations. Other ways of life, other social conventions and other cultural traditions are subordinated to the transnationalist world view. As globalization has picked up speed in the last twenty years the liquidation of non-European, non-capitalist ways of life seems much closer to completion. Expressed more skeptically, globalization is the latest phase of imperialist colonization. Visions of economic life at odds with the hegemonic European outlook are disappearing, and were it not for the grandiose claims of so many economists, business leaders, politicians and journalists, this disturbing demise of humankind's rich cultural heritage and diversity would be brought to our attention much more regularly.

Nevertheless, it is possible to speak much more specifically about the standardization of life around the world. The homogenization of culture—of music, art, the media, food and so forth—is unmistakable, but more than anything else globalization standardizes working life and its daily rhythms. Globalization is the spread of the art of "making a living," of wage work and its familiar routines. Although we are more likely to hear about the spread of Western culture, it is the extension of Western capitalism's run-of-the-mill customs regarding working life that is uprooting local traditions more than anything else. Around the world daily life is infused with the habits of the wage earner and, in this way, the character of daily life looks remarkably similar whether one is in Manilla or Lima, Saint John or St. John's. Life as a wage earner in capitalism is simple: one works for a wage, usually during the best part of the day, and those wages are used to procure the necessities of life. And as the loss of access to land intensifies around the world, wage work becomes the only means to survival. It is telling that good fortune is measured by the ability to secure work in our globalizing world, and for many would-be wage earners the struggle to find work never ends. In the shanty towns of the South, the innercities of North America, and chronically depressed regions such as the Miramichi in New Brunswick and the north of Cape Breton Island, job opportunities are uncommon and a person's identity can be consumed by their bleak job prospects and the fear of long-term hardship. Understandably, the most common way of thinking about ourselves is as employed or unemployed—not happy or unhappy, not Christian or Muslim, not good or bad—but rather as a person who is working or one who is desperately in need of work.

The split between the employed and the unemployed is critical to understanding the nature of globalization. Equally important is the distinction between good jobs and bad jobs. Not all jobs in the capitalist world are alike. Workplace experiences, conditions and struggles can vary widely, and although all workers are vulnerable to a degree, some are much more so than others. Jeffery Harrod has elaborated on this important distinction between working people who are relatively protected by institutionalized labour laws and labour practices and those who are relatively exposed.

> The division between the unprotected worker and the established worker, as with all relations based on power, is one of degree and is open to dispute. At the ends of the extreme, however, the situation is very clear. In the bipartite social relations of the auto industry in the United States in the 1970s or the enterprise corporatist relations of Japanese enterprises, the bulk of the workers were protected from dismissal for life, surrounded by laws, practices, and constraints against employers' power.... [At the other end of the spectrum is] the casual worker in a third-world city who is at the mercy of the casual employer of labour and can never expect the state, union, or other worker organization to prevent the most dire economic and physical abuse. (1987: 39–40)

The distinction between the "protected worker" and the "exposed worker," however, does not map onto geographical divisions between the so-called industrialized economies of the North and societies in the South. Protected and unprotected workers permeate the Atlantic region; "good jobs" and "bad jobs" exist side by side. We see a large number of workers who are shielded by unions and an array of labour laws developed during the twentieth century. We also see workers who lack basic protections in their day-to-day work, who are poorly paid and who often feel extremely vulnerable to the whims of their employers.

The established or relatively protected worker in Atlantic Canada is the focus of this chapter. To understand his or her struggle it must be recalled that an important element of globalization—arguably its defining feature—has been the assault on the protected worker throughout the North. When the profitability crunch arrived in the late 1960s, the Fordist labour regime stood in the way of downward wage reform. Indeed, the Fordist labour regime was institutionally embedded to the extent that Northern societies occasionally saw formal rounds of public policy consultations between the state, organized labour and capital in the post-Second World War period. Over the last three decades, however, the minions of capital have been determined to roll back the Fordist labour regime and open the class compact in the North in order to establish a *modus vivendi* more favourable to capital. Ousting the socially and legally entrenched Fordist labour regime has demanded creative measures. Within government, in the media, in declarations of the business community, in economic think-tanks and in the academy the basic elements that coalesced to create the Fordist worker have been attacked, re-examined and re-formulated. In a little more than two decades, the Fordist worker—a wage worker who toils for a set number of hours each week and perhaps grabs a bit of overtime; who enjoys a decent wage in exchange for an honest day's work; whose burdens are eased by a respectable array of social programs and decent benefits packages; whose children expect a life as good as that of their parents, and perhaps even a better one; who can count on decades of loyal service to his or her employer; and who is protected by strong labour laws—has withered to an official anachronism. The "noble toiler" has been replaced by the flexiworker—an "associate" who must continually upgrade skills for the new economy; multitask inside the firm; be willing to pass through several careers over the course of adulthood; strive to be self-sufficient; expect little assistance from the state; be adaptable and flexible; and, most importantly, simply be grateful for work.

The extent to which Canada's working people have internalized this public elaboration of the "new" worker is open to question. Nevertheless, it is clear that the business community at least has successfully shifted public discourse to the right, given the fact that it has accomplished some of its objectives without working people pouring back into the streets. This right-wing discourse permeates all levels of discussion and dupes many. The corporate world has adroitly framed issues in terms that necessitate business-friendly conclusions. Of course, many of the strategies of capital have been less refined, especially those that have simply shifted productive operations to the South to take advantage of cheaper labour.

In the end, the Fordist worker has taken a direct hit. After three decades, the Fordist labour regime is frayed, and irregular and fragmented roll-backs are commonplace. The challenge in this chapter is to explore the extent of this hit on the Fordist worker in Atlantic Canada. This historic assault registers in stalled rates of unionization across the region, precipitous declines in union militancy, stagnating real wages in every province and an atrophy in regional labour laws. A renewed class war has been under way in Atlantic Canada for two decades, and its manifestation is readily apparent when the fate of the Fordist worker is examined a little more closely.

The Stagnation in Unionization Rates

To unpack the effects of globalization on the Fordist worker in Atlantic Canada it is helpful to review the basic profile of the regional economy. As Table 2.1 shows, the Atlantic Canadian economy is now dominated by the service-producing sector. This is consistent with historic employment trends in the twentieth century, trends that saw declines in agricultural employment and relative rises in manufacturing over the first half of the century and unprecedented growth in the service sector in the last half of the century. By the year 2000, the service sector in Atlantic Canada employed more than two thirds of the region's working people. Service-producing employment ranges from 63.1 percent in Prince Edward Island up to 69.5 percent in Newfoundland and Labrador. The goods-producing sector accounted for slightly less than 20 percent of the region's employment, while 13.5 percent of Atlantic Canadians worked for themselves. Each province evinces a similar profile in terms of the relative distribution of the goods-producing and service-producing sectors. It is also clear that the goods-producing sector, which includes manufacturing, forestry, mining, oil and gas, construction, utilities and agriculture, is concentrated in Nova Scotia and New Brunswick. The largest goods-producing base relative to the overall size of the provincial economy is in New Brunswick, where 22.1 percent of all workers work in a goods-producing industry.

Unionization rates in Atlantic Canada vary slightly from province to province. The unionization rate of Newfoundland and Labrador's goods-producing sector, although small in terms of the total number of workers

Table 2.1
Overview of Atlantic Canadian Economy 2000
Working People/Sectoral Size/Unionization

	Total Number of Workers	Goods producing Sector	% of Total	% in Unions	Service Producing Sector	% of Total	% in unions	Self-employed	%
Atlantic Canada	1,023,700	198,600	19.4	31.2	687,200	67.1	31.8	137,900	13.5
Newfound-land and Labrador	205,200	35,800	17.4	45.5	142,600	69.5	37.5	26,800	13.1
Nova Scotia	419,600	76,500	18.2	26.4	284,700	67.9	31.2	58,400	13.9
P.E.I.	64,500	12,400	19.2	16.1	40,700	63.1	33.2	11,400	17.7
New Brunswick	334,400	73,900	22.1	31.8	219,200	65.6	28.6	41,300	12.4

Source: Canada, Statistics Canada, CANSIM II

throughout the region, is the highest in Canada at 45.5 percent, as is its rate of 37.5 percent in the service sector. Prince Edward Island's unioniza-tion rate of 16.1 percent in its goods sector was the lowest rate in the region. Outside of Newfoundland and Labrador, however, the rates of unionization throughout the region tend to hover around 30 percent; the two exceptions to this trend are noteworthy. Nova Scotia's goods-produc-ing sector, which accounts for 38.5 percent of the entire region's employ-ment in the goods sector, stood at just 26.4 percent in 2000. And, in sharp contrast to its low unionization rate in the goods-producing sector, Prince Edward Island's service sector rate of 33.2 percent was the second highest in Atlantic Canada.

With this snapshot of the relative sizes and rates of unionization across the region, attention can be turned to the changes in unionization rates over the last twenty-five years. Figure 2.1 reveals that rates of unionization across the region levelled off during the 1980s and early 1990s. It is clear that the overall rates of unionization in the Atlantic provinces were fairly stable and that this trend was comparable with the rest of Canada. In New Brunswick, for example, the average rate of unionization between 1976 and 1985 was 35.5 percent, and in the next decade the average rate stood at 36.4 percent, a variation of less than 1 percent. Similarly, in Nova Scotia, the average overall rate of unionization for the same periods were 31.5 percent and 32.4 percent respectively, also a variation of less than 1 percent. In Newfoundland and Labrador, a much higher rate of overall unionization is immediately evident. In 1984, the

Figure 2.1
Stagnation in Atlantic Canadian Union Diversity

Source: *Canada, Statistics Canada,* CANSIM II

Figure 2.2
Union Attrition in Late 1990s

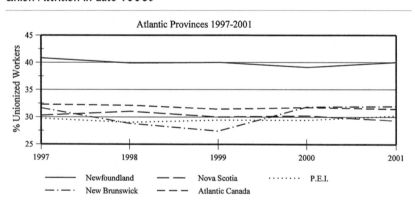

Source: *Canada, Statistics Canada,* CANSIM II

province climbed to a rate of 57.4 percent. This rate, however, fell off in later years and was as low as 50.1 percent in 1987. Between 1986 and 1995 Newfoundland and Labrador's overall rate of unionization, although still the highest in Canada, stabilized at a yearly average of 53.6 percent.

The relatively stable rates of unionization between the mid-1970s and the mid-1990s persisted between 1997 and 2001. Due to changes in the data collection procedures at Statistics Canada, the rates in Figures 2.1 and 2.2 are not comparable, and there is no data available for 1996. Nevertheless, the trends are once again clear. The rates of unionization in the latter part of the 1990s reveal slight declines. Across the region the

Figure 2.3
Unionization Declines in the Traditional Economy

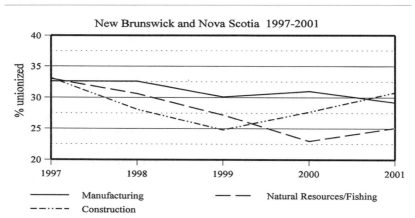

Source: *Calculated from Canada, Statistics Canada,* CANSIM II

overall rate of unionization fell from 32.3 percent to 31.4 percent between 1997 and 2001. The greatest decline was in New Brunswick, where the overall rate of unionization wobbled downwards from 30.1 percent in 1997 to 28.8 percent in 2001. In Nova Scotia the overall rate of unionization fell from 30.3 percent to 29.3 percent over the same five-year period. The slight variations that appear over any given period do not permit us to speak definitively about declining rates of unionization in Atlantic Canada, especially when some declines have been much more pronounced in other Northern countries, especially the United States. Nevertheless, Figures 2.1 and 2.2 reveal that the rates of unionization in the Atlantic Canadian provinces have stagnated in the last two decades, arresting the historic rise in unionization rates in North America in the earlier decades of the twentieth century.

It is also noteworthy that the rate of unionization in the traditional economies of Nova Scotia and New Brunswick do appear to be in decline. As Figure 2.3 shows, the rate of unionization in the manufacturing sector in these two provinces declined from 32.6 percent in 1997 to 29.2 percent in 2001. In Nova Scotia, the province with the largest manufacturing base in the region, union density fell from 32.2 percent to 26.6 percent in five years. Even sharper declines appear in the natural resource sector of Nova Scotia and New Brunswick. Between 1997 and 2001 the union density rate in the natural resource sector fell from 33 percent to 25.1 percent. The construction sector also evinced rather sharp declines after 1997, falling from 33.1 percent to 30.8 percent by 2001. Indeed, by 2001 only about one in four workers was unionized in the natural resource sector in Nova Scotia and New Brunswick, and only about three in ten workers were unionized in the manufacturing and construction sectors. Once again, such sharp declines might be exaggerated by virtue of the smaller overall numbers of workers in each sector and by the variations that can occur within shorter periods of time. The trends are nevertheless consistent with the overall stagnation in union density that has beset the region. Of course, it is possible that we may be witnessing the beginnings of a historic reversal in unionization rates in Atlantic Canada, a reversal that has certainly been witnessed in other countries.

We can be sure that union growth has been arrested in Atlantic Canada over the last two decades, a fact which is consistent with our expectations about the effects of globalization and the neoliberal culture of austerity. However, if we were to leave off with this important observation, our story about union stagnation in Atlantic Canada would be incomplete. What is clear from a closer examination of the information is that some sectors of the economy in Atlantic Canada have stagnated at extremely low rates of unionization. At first glance, rates of unionization appear to be frozen in Atlantic Canada at around 30 percent. This figure, however, is misleading because union density rates are sectorally stratified. In those service sectors linked to the historic expansion of the state in the twentieth century, particularly public administration, education and health care, rates of unionization exceed 50 percent. Outside of these sectors, however, rates of unionization begin to fall precipitously. As indicated in Figure 2.4, a second tier of the economy, including many of the traditional goods-producing industries, such as manufacturing, forestry and mining, are unionized at a rate of about 30 percent in Atlantic Canada. A large portion of the economy (primarily service workers outside of the fields of government work, health care and education) is unionized at rates in and around 10 percent, however. To the extent that one associates the typical Fordist worker with organized labour, he or she appears to endure in only a few sectors of the economy and shows little sign of surfacing to any significant degree in much of the service economy in the near future.

It is helpful to address each province in a little more detail. The overall rate of unionization in Newfoundland and Labrador was 40 percent in 2001. Its union density rate of 38.5 percent in 2001 across the entire service sector was the highest in the region. The service sector accounts for more than three quarters of the province's employment. Workers in public administration, health care and education, the three sectors directly linked to the growth of the Keynesian welfare state during the twentieth century, were unionized at an impressive rate of 70.8 percent. In the goods-producing sector, the rate of unionization of 46 percent was also very high when compared with the rest of the region and, indeed, all of Canada. Outside of these sectors, however, union density changes abruptly. The rate of unionization among service sector workers outside

Figure 2.4
Sectorally Stratified Unionization Rates
Atlantic Canada 2001

Unionization in State Sector
Public Administration, Health Care and Education

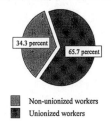

Non-unionized workers
Unionized workers

■ The rate of unionization in the state sector, which grew in the 20th century, is relatively high—65.7 percent across the region

■ Almost 7 of every 10 workers in education, health care and public administration are protected by a union

Unionization in Goods Economy

■ Unionization in the goods-producing sector is much lower—just 32.0 percent, which is down from 33.5 percent in 1997

■ Only 3 of every 10 workers in agriculture, natural resources, fishing, utilities, construction and manufacturing are protected by a union

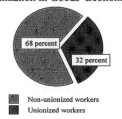

Non-unionized workers
Unionized workers

Service Sector Rates Beyond State Sector

Non-unionized Workers
Unionized Workers

■ Among service sector workers outside the state sector rates of unionization falls precipitously to just 11.1 percent

■ Almost 9 of every 10 service workers outside the state sector do not have a union buffer in the workplace

Source: Canada, Statistics Canada, CANSIM II

the fields of public administration, health care and education was just 15.1 percent in 2001. Moreover, the rate of unionization in the accommodation and food service industry—the backbone of the tourist industry—was just 11.2 percent. As these last figures reveal, very few service sector workers outside of the fields of public administration, health care and education are unionized, and these workers accounted for almost 60 percent of all workers in the service sector and 46 percent of all Newfoundland and Labrador workers in 2001.

Similarly revealing pictures of sectorally stratified rates of unionization are evident in the other three Atlantic provinces. In Nova Scotia, service workers constituted 79 percent of the work force, excluding the self-employed, in 2001. The overall rate of union density among the service workers in that year was 29.8 percent. The rate of unionization among workers in the goods-producing sector in 2001 was 27.5 percent, down from 33.9 percent in 1997. Among public administration, health care and education workers the rate of unionization climbed to 66.7 percent. Outside of these three fields, however, the rate of unionization plummets to 10.4 percent. These figures indicate that although service workers outside the provincial state's administrative and social sector numbered about 189,000 workers in 2001, and comprised about 65 percent of all service workers in Nova Scotia, nine out of ten did not belong to a union. Moreover, in the province's restaurant and hotel industry the rate of unionization stood at a meagre 7.3 percent in 2001.

Prince Edward Island's service sector workers accounted for more than 75 percent of all employment in the province in 2001. The union density rate in the island's service industry was 34 percent in 2001, up slightly from 32.9 percent in 1997. In contrast, workers in the goods-producing sector were unionized at a rate of 17.7 percent in 2001. When we peer inside the service sector, however, a highly stratified picture again forms. As in Newfoundland and Labrador and Nova Scotia, Prince Edward Island workers in public administration, health care and education were unionized at a very high rate—71.2 percent. Service workers outside of these fields, who comprise six out of every ten service workers on the island, were unionized at the low rate of only 7.6 percent. Worse still, rates of unionization in the accommodation and food service industry, a sector that has boomed with the construction of the Confederation Bridge, were so low that they did not register in the data.

Finally, in New Brunswick, the rate of unionization in the service sector in 2001 was 27.9 percent, down slightly from a rate of 29.6 percent in 1997. The province had a comparable rate of 31.9 percent in its goods sector in 2001. The rate of unionization in the state's administrative and social sector was 62.2 percent. Beyond government workers, educators and health care workers, however, the rate of unionization fell precipitously to just 8.6 percent. Even this very low rate of unionization among New Brunswick's remaining service sector workers had fallen off from the rate of 9 percent in 1997. This low union density in 2001 applied to about two thirds of all service sector workers in the province, numbering about 144,000 wage earners or almost half the total work force. In the hotel and restaurant industry, the rate of unionization was only 4.5 percent in 2001. In New Brunswick's managerial and administrative sector, a grouping of enterprises that includes the province's celebrated call centres, unionization rates were less than 1 percent in 2001.

Two observations regarding the fate of the Fordist worker are inescapable. First, globalization appears to have stagnated unionization in sectors that once boasted formidable unions, especially the public sector and segments of the traditional goods-producing economy. The fate of these sectors, therefore, will be linked to the strength of the Fordist labour regime in the short and medium terms. In Atlantic Canada, attacks on the size of government and the contraction of segments of the traditional economy will combine to threaten protected workers across the region. In other words, union densities are never locked, and the evolution of these sectors will affect the future of workers who are already protected.

The general political and economic climate in Atlantic Canada also militates against the organization of working people in sectors that have had a robust union presence in the past. Stories about layoffs, unemployment trends, plant closures, rising poverty, lockouts and busted unions enhance the malaise among working people in the era of globalization. The neoliberal culture of austerity claims that everyone must make do with less, that governments are going broke, that welfare recipients are a drain on society, that the health care system is too costly and, more vaguely, that globalization means that nobody's job is really secure. Workers fear the loss of their jobs more than ever, and this means that many workers fear the effects of a union presence in the workplace. It is not the union that workers fear, but rather the possibility of a harsh response from employers when their firm is unionized, responses that can range from punishing pro-union employees—through a cut in hours, supervisory harassment, demotion, layoffs and so forth—to the outright closure of the workplace.

Indeed, the worker-unfriendly realities of neoliberalism will undermine efforts to unionize workers even when workplace abuses run deep. Anxiety and vulnerability can have a profound effect on the unfolding drama of the workplace. A rare glimpse of this relationship is offered in Shaun Comish's (1993) account of the May 9, 1992, explosion that tore through the Westray mine in Plymouth, Nova Scotia. Comish details a litany of managerial disregard for workers' safety in the mine, systematic violation of provincial mining standards, aggressive verbal abuse from management, insufficient training of new workers, dismissal of workers' suggestions to improve mine safety, managerial indifference to chronic stress among the miners and even the failure to respect rudimentary workplace standards such as the provision of proper lunch breaks over long shifts. Comish writes about the daily torment of work in the mine, and about his efforts to relieve the anxiety:

> Many times I went back to Len's house—that is where I stayed—
> and sat there with a coffee, thinking, "I can't do this any more."
> After mulling it over for a while, I would go across the street, call
> home and tell my wife that I was going to quit. She would always
> be understanding because she knows me well enough to know
> that I don't scare easy. I have worked in some pretty crazy places,
> but I had never complained to her before about any place except

Westray. She would usually say something like "If it's that bad, quit, come home and we will work it out after." I have never been a quitter, so each time I would think to myself that maybe I was just overtired or cranky and it will probably be better tomorrow. That tomorrow never did come. (1993: 21–22)

Indeed, the miners were so fearful concerning their working conditions that they made promises to each other to reveal the truth about the mine in the event of a disaster.

It was when we were working in these sorts of conditions that we made pacts with each other. If anything ever happened and one of us died, the other would make sure the reason was found out. Lenny and I talked about this many, many times at work and at home. It was really quite awful being that nervous and worried that you might be killed at work some day. (1993: 26)

Comish's effort to convince himself that his fears were exaggerated reveals the effects of the culture of austerity on the way in which workers understand labour markets:

A lot of people ask me why we kept working there. I guess the only answer I can give is that nowadays when you have a job it is very scary to quit and hope to get a job somewhere else. I often felt that maybe things would get better someday. Some guys who worked at Westray didn't really know anything else but mining. That's all they had ever done and probably all they ever will do. The promise of fifteen years of steady work weighed heavy on your mind. (1993: 28)

Simply walking away from the job was not an option: "This abusive treatment was tolerated," Comish stresses, "because of the lack of other jobs to go to" (1993: 55). In the face of the constant abuse and perilous workplace conditions efforts were afoot to form a union, but workers were fearful. Management at the mine tried to undercut the efforts to organize with promises to improve safety and provide bonuses for the workers. But as efforts to unionize moved forward the company began to intimidate open supporters of the union. In a generalized atmosphere of fear and vulnerability this intimidation slowed the organization efforts down considerably. "A lot of the workforce," Comish wrote, "were still nervous about signing a card or getting involved" (1993: 31).

The second, more specific observation about union stagnation in Atlantic Canada is that it extends to sectors in which worker protections afforded by unions are negligible. Globalization and its worker-unfriendly neoliberal agenda has helped to halt the unionization in the service sector of the economy—one that, in terms of its treatment of workers, has "nowhere to go but up." Of course, factors such as high employee turnover, youthfulness and the seasonal nature of some service sector work will also figure into the low rate of unionization. Managers and owners ill-disposed to having a union in their place of business—and this includes most of them—are bound to feel vindicated by the general hostility towards unions that is very much a part of the neoliberal agenda. The withering of the Fordist worker, anticipated by an understanding of globalization that acknowledges the desire of capitalists to roll back the historic class compact of the twentieth century, has been achieved, in part, by preventing the spread of unions in the service producing sector of the economy.

Labour Militancy During the Transition to Globalization

The Fordist worker has been under assault and understandably fears for the future. Organized labour everywhere has been passing through a difficult period of concessionary bargaining in the face of incessant corporate and political threats. In this neoliberal era, the mere presence of an organized workplace seems to invite exaggerated ridicule from politicians and corporate interests, who attack the very idea of collective worker resistance and solidarity with an array of ideological mechanisms. The message directed at today's working people is relentlessly hostile—workers should be grateful if they have a full-time job; workers often lack sufficient skills and experience; workers are greedy when measured against their counterparts in other countries; unions have behaved irresponsibly in the past; Canadians have come to expect too much from the Canadian state; and everyone must expect less in these hard times. It is reasonable to assume that significant chunks of this unfriendly message have lodged themselves in the thoughts and understandings of everyone.

A more worker-sensitive message does not circulate widely enough, especially in the media, to counteract these negative characterizations. It is rare to hear more measured assessments of workers and their jobs. We almost never hear about the deteriorating conditions of many workplaces; the vastness of worker know-how and skill; the stagnation in wages across the country or below-subsistence wages across the South; the historically important role of unions in safeguarding wages; and the obligations of the Canadian state that arose out of the worker protests and sacrifices of the first half of the twentieth century. The tireless efforts to sustain a worker-friendly message by numerous labour federations and unions in Canada have not successfully counteracted this negativity. We hear much more about workers "taking" than we do about them "giving," a claim that flips an elementary truth of capitalism on its head, and one that is at least as bold as it is wrong.

Moreover, as unions struggle to finesse their way through an economic agenda set by transnational capital, many labour leaders have become unwitting accomplices in the attack on working people. Over the last two decades some have called for wage moderation, accepted the basic principles of debt management, shared the view that social programs had to be restructured, endorsed measures to "strengthen the Canadian economy," and embraced a state-driven "training" agenda that translates job cuts and chronic unemployment into issues about worker skill and knowledge. The right-wing shift in public policy discourse often traps those who work tirelessly on behalf of working people.

To compound matters, many workers have had first-hand acquaintance with the hardships imposed on working people over the last two decades. The feeling persists that difficulties can arise out of nowhere and that no one can be entirely sure about the future. Working people can become trapped in a sort of existential bind where they feel frustrated and bitterly disappointed with their jobs on one hand, yet relieved that they even have a job on the other. In this culture of austerity working people are wary, cautious and less disposed to pressing hard for better working conditions and higher wages.

In this climate it is a challenge to find statistical measurements that will reflect the anxieties and fears of the rank and file as well as those of union leaders, who have been overwhelmed with conflicting messages about the course of the global economy, who have been threatened with job cuts and plant closures, and who have been confronted repeatedly with demands for concessions from managers and owners. Information on strikes and lockouts can provide some indication as to how working people and their union leaders feel in the neoliberal era. It is an axiom of labour relations in North America that union militancy tends to decline in tough times and rise when the economy strengthens. Union leaders seem to calculate that it is prudent not to push too hard when times are tough. In the present atmosphere of uncertainty, therefore, we should expect to see a corresponding decline in union militancy. The discipline imposed by the global economy, along with the ever-pressing discourse about austerity and sacrifice, is bound to temper demands and make unions more inclined, reluctantly to be sure, to accept the concessions forced on them by employers. In the language of contemporary social analysis, union leaders and many of the rank and file have internalized the message of restraint and self-discipline in this general climate of neoliberal austerity.

Adding to these anxieties is the prevailing notion that we live in tough times, irrespective of the performance of the economy. So many economic reports in the popular media seem designed to brace workers for more bad news down the line. A sort of recessionary psyche has set in, and for working people this general outlook is vindicated by stories of mass layoffs and plant closures. In light of this, we should expect to see a decline in the higher-order confrontations between workers and their employers. The number of strikes should fall, and as union members accept the concessions forced on them by their employers, there should be fewer confrontations leading to a lockout. Short of extensive interviews with working people themselves, the frequency of strikes and lockouts should help measure the real impact of globalization and the neoliberal agenda in Atlantic Canada. And, indeed, they do.

The militancy of organized workers declined precipitously over the last two decades. Table 2.2 shows steep declines in the number of strikes and lockouts in the private sector in Atlantic Canada between 1977 and 2000. Between 1977 and 1981, the region averaged fifty-two strikes each year. Over the next nine years the average number of strikes each year fell to forty. During the next decade the average number of strikes dropped off to just nineteen each year. It is revealing to compare the private sector in the first five years after 1977 with the last five years up to the year 2000. Between 1977 and 1981, that is, during the early phase of the transition from the Fordist order to the post-Fordist order, the average number of strikes exceeded fifty per year. In the five years at the end of our survey period, however, the average number of strikes and lockouts in any given year plummeted to just seventeen. The congealing of the neoliberal order over the last decade has been accompanied by a precipitous decline in union militancy, regardless of the undulating performance of the Atlantic Canadian economy.

The sharpest declines in strikes and lockouts are evident in New Brunswick. This province averaged thirty strikes each year in the private sector between 1977 and 1981. Over the next decade that number would fall to just seventeen strikes each year in the private sector. During the 1990s, labour disruptions bottomed out altogether as the average number of strikes and lockouts in any given year fell to five. In the last five years the average number of strikes has fallen to just three each year, a figure suggestive of a complete collapse of labour militancy in the province. New Brunswick had seen as many as forty-six labour disruptions in the private sector in 1978, and another forty-seven in 1981. In stark contrast, the province saw only two disruptions each year in 1997 and 1998. In 1980 New Brunswick officially lost 157,630 person days to strikes and lockouts, but in 1998 only 8,740 person days were lost. In the last two decades the province has experienced more than a seventy-five percent decline in strikes and lockouts.

Steep declines in strikes and lockouts in the private sector are also evident in Nova Scotia and Newfoundland and Labrador. The latter province averaged twenty-five strikes and lockouts per year in the latter part of the 1970s. In 1978 alone, there were thirty-one labour disruptions, and this number peaked in 1980 at thirty-three. Over the remainder of the

Table 2.2
Strikes and Lockouts in Atlantic Canada
Private and Public Sectors 1977–2000

Year	Newfoundland		Prince Edward Island		Nova Scotia		New Brunswick	
	Private	Public	Private	Public	Private	Public	Private	Public
1977	23	16	0	0	19	3	19	11
1978	31	5	2	0	16	11	46	8
1979	24	9	3	0	20	14	24	6
1980	33	7	2	0	19	7	18	7
1981	17	15	5	0	16	37	47	12
1982	14	4	2	0	11	4	24	6
1983	16	5	0	0	10	2	7	5
1984	12	4	0	0	8	3	11	14
1985	8	8	1	1	16	5	14	7
1986	14	5	0	0	8	14	21	2
1987	14	0	0	0	6	1	20	6
1988	10	1	0	0	7	6	19	2
1989	14	5	0	0	12	4	19	2
1990	11	12	0	0	18	10	19	1
1991	9	4	0	0	7	6	10	2
1992	7	1	0	0	19	1	7	6
1993	8	2	0	1	7	2	5	0
1994	9	2	0	0	7	0	9	3
1995	7	3	1	0	10	1	6	1
1996	10	2	1	0	9	2	4	0
1997	5	0	0	0	4	1	2	0
1998	6	6	0	0	6	8	2	0
1999	13	3	0	0	9	9	5	3
2000	5	8	0	0	4	1	3	1

Source: Adapted from Human Resources and Development Canada, Workplace Information Directorate 2001

1980s, however, the number of strikes and lockouts fell to roughly twelve in any given year. And over the next decade that figure would decline to just seven labour disruptions each year in the private sector. The province that regularly saw more than twenty formal labour disruptions a year in the late 1970s experienced as few as five strikes or lockouts in 1997 and again in 2000. A similar pattern of steep decline is evident in Nova Scotia over the last two decades. Nova Scotia fell from an average of eighteen strikes and lockouts each year between 1977 and 1981 to an average of only ten per year during the 1980s. For most of the 1990s Nova Scotia averaged only eight strikes each year, and between 1996 and 2000 the province saw just six strikes on average in any given year. Underscoring this decline is the fact that the province experienced twenty labour disruptions in 1979 and only four in 1997. On the whole, strikes and lockouts in the region's largest economy fell by more than half as the post-Fordist social and political framework took hold; and this decline persisted, regardless of the performance of the economy. Even in Prince Edward Island, there was a handful of labour disruptions in the private sector each year during the late 1970s and, in stark contrast, long stretches without a single strike or lockout throughout the 1990s.

The decline of labour militancy across the region is equally evident in the public sector. A glance at Table 2.2 shows the plunge in the number of strikes and lockouts over the last twenty years. In 1977, for example, there were thirty labour disruptions in the public sector. Twenty years later there was only one labour disruption in the public sector throughout the entire region. All provinces experienced a sharp decline in labour militancy in the public sector. In Newfoundland and Labrador there was an average of ten strikes each year in the public sector in the late 1970s. This figure fell to just six each year on average in the 1980s, and declined further in the 1990s to just three strikes per year. In 1977 there were sixteen labour disruptions in the public sector and another fifteen in 1981. Between 1992 and 1997, in contrast, there was only ten strikes in Newfoundland and Labrador's public sector in total. Sharp declines were also evident in New Brunswick, where an average of eight labour disruptions in the public sector in the late 1970s fell to six each year during the 1980s and to between only one and two each year during the 1990s. Indeed, in New Brunswick the total number of strikes between 1993 and 2000 did not rise above the number of strikes in either 1977, 1981 or 1984. A slightly less steep decline is evident in Nova Scotia. The average yearly number of strikes of nine in the late 1970s fell to eight each year during the 1980s, and then to just four each year during the 1990s. A province that had experienced as many as thirty-seven labour disruptions in the public sector in 1981 alone saw only one strike in 1992, one in 1995, one in 1997 and one in 2000.

To the extent that labour unrest is a function of job security, rising as workers gain confidence and security and falling when workers are unsure about their future, we might expect the decline in labour disruptions in the public sector to be a little less pronounced. Although the overall number of strikes is greater in the private sector in most years, this expectation is not confirmed by our numbers. Figure 2.5 indicates the similarities between private and public sectors throughout the region. Both sectors tend to rise or fall in unison, and the downward shift in both is equally palpable. Similar trends were also evident in each province. In Newfoundland and Labrador, for example, labour disruptions in the 1980s and 1990s fell by 72 percent in the private sector and 70 percent in the public sector Canada. In New Brunswick, private sector labour dis-

Figure 2.5
Declining Strikes and Lockouts in Atlantic Canada

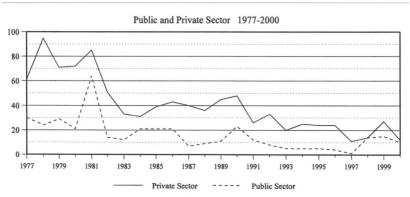

Public and Private Sector 1977-2000

———— Private Sector   - - - - - Public Sector

Source: Adapted from Human Resources and Development Canada, Workplace Information Directorate 2001

ruptions declined by 83 percent in the private sector and 81 percent in the public sector over the same period (adapted from Human Resources and Development Canada, Workplace Information Directorate 2001). Nova Scotia reveals the largest differential between private sector and public sector declines, where the private sector fell by 66 percent in the last two decades while the public sector declined by only 55 percent (adapted from Human Resources and Development Canada, Workplace Information Directorate 2001). Although the declines in labour disruptions in the public service are always slightly less than those in the private sector, it would seem that years of "worker bashing" by politicians and commentators throughout Canada, the looming prospect of government downsizing, wage freezes, forced contracts, program cuts and the cumulative effects of the culture of austerity have taken a toll on public sector workers. Sustained confrontations with employers now seem as unpalatable to public sector workers in Atlantic Canada as they are to their private sector counterparts.

The general decline of labour disruptions in both the private and public sectors in Atlantic Canada is summarized in Figure 2.6. In 1978, for example, there were 119 strikes or lockouts in the region and a high of 149 labour disruptions in 1981. In 1997 there were only twelve recorded labour interruptions across the region. There was a hint that strikes and lockouts might be rising in the latter part of the 1990s. In 1999, for example, the region saw forty-two labour disruptions. However, the next year that figure fell back to twenty-two, the second lowest number of strikes and lockouts in the last twenty-five years.

Clearly, the collapse of formal labour militancy in Atlantic Canada in

Figure 2.6
The Collapse of Formal Labour Militancy

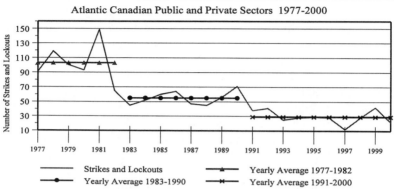

Atlantic Canadian Public and Private Sectors 1977-2000

Source: Adapted from Human Resources and Development Canada, Workplace Information Directorate 2001

the last two decades has been extensive. It might be said that a forced labour calm has settled over the region. The explanation for the peaceful appearance of labour relations in recent years is undoubtedly the result of fear—the fear of losing a job, of losing the ability to support a family and of losing the dignity that comes with full-time employment. Workers have strategically pulled back from the inevitable confrontations with their employers. Union leaders have calculated that it is better to tread lightly during contract negotiations than push hard for higher wages and better working conditions, to relax their demands rather than risk managerial or corporate reprisals such as lockouts, layoffs and plant closures. They are regularly reminded by employers that if they take a tough line during contract talks, or if they seriously threaten to strike, the economic well-being of the enterprise could be imperilled and its ability to remain competitive in an integrated global economy irreparably undermined. The argument is straightforward: higher labour costs lead to competitive disadvantages, which could very well lead to the failure of the firm. From the perspective of worried labour negotiators, negotiators who are also familiar with the rash of layoffs and plant closures across Canada over the last few decades, the corporate threat often has just enough plausibility to force concessions. Labour leaders also realize that if they disregard such corporate blackmail and persevere on behalf of the rank and file, leading the union in the direction of a strike, they must face an unsympathetic public conditioned by years of anti-union calumny, as well as the possibility that their employer will hire scabs in the event of a strike.

The prospect of a long and fruitless strike preys upon the minds of union negotiators throughout the region. Recent labour relations in Atlantic Canada have unfolded in the shadow of the Irving Oil Refinery strike, which occurred in Saint John in the mid-1990s. The bitter strike lasted more than two years, and included frequent court challenges, the use of scabs, co-workers breaking ranks and returning to work, supportive rallies, public appeals, terrible stress for the striking workers and, finally, public humiliation for those who stuck it out. The strike ended only when the remaining members of Local 691 of the Communications, Energy and Paperworkers union voted to accept a punitive contract that sacked the entire local executive and sent much of the rank and file off for weeks of ideological reconditioning.[1] The back of the union had been broken. When the strike concluded in mid-August of 1996, CBC Radio's *World at Six* program identified it as a formative moment in contemporary labour relations in Canada, and speculated openly about the harm that such a devastating strike might have on organized labour across the country. Undoubtedly, the affair cast a pall over labour relations in Atlantic Canada.

Considering the impact of the Irving Oil Refinery strike, especially its open attacks on worker solidarity and collective worker action, brings to mind other decisive strikes in North American labour history. In his concluding reflections on the effects of the strike in 1892 between the Carnegie Steel Company and the Amalgamated Association of Iron and Steel Workers, Authur G. Burgoyne's (1971: 296–98) observations seem as applicable to the Irving strike as they did to the strike in Homestead, Pennsylvania, more than a century ago:

> Although ignobly routed in the courts, the Carnegie Company lost not a foot of the ground gained at Homestead. On the contrary, it has since doubly re-enforced itself, for not only is the spirit of unionism stamped out among the employees of the firm, but fully three-fourths of the former union men are now working, most of them at their old jobs, without exhibiting a trace of the independence which was once their pride, or making any pretensions to a voice in the determination of their wages.... The active leaders of the strike were, of course, excluded from the amnesty, and few of them have since been able to secure employment at their trade.... If there are grievances to be suffered the men must simply be contented to suffer them in silence rather than invite a repetition of the calamitous consequences of their first and only encounter with Chairman Frick [of Carnegie Steel].

Labour leaders are well aware of the fact that they take a risk when accepting concessions. In addition to exacerbating tensions between the leadership and the rank and file, there is always the underlying fear that employers may exaggerate tales about their corporate health or their competitive predicament to gain unfair advantage in bargaining. Worse still, a firm's decision to close or re-locate may have very little to do with the nature of labour relations. Union leaders can never really know for sure. In the end, a history of peaceful labour relations does not protect workers from harsh managerial decisions. The fate of the Lantic Sugar workers, also in Saint John, reminds us that relatively calm labour relations might be factored into decisions to close plants. For decades the sugar-producing facility was a fixture on the port city's horizon, and over the years generations of workers had been producing assorted sugars for the Canadian market. The workers were unionized, well-paid and, they believed, in reasonably secure positions. In the context of this study, they epitomized Fordist workers, buffered by a union and protected by an array of labour relations conventions and legal statutes. Over the years their relations with Lantic had been relatively peaceful, and the one strike in recent memory had been uneventful. In the late 1990s, however, the workers at Lantic Sugar were given shocking news. Lantic management was planning to close its Saint John facility. According to management, it had become too costly to operate facilities in both Saint John and in Montreal. Ironically, some of the Lantic workers strongly suspected that the history of relative labour peace at the Saint John facility was decisive in their misfortune. Management, they believed, was not sure that the cessation of operations in Montreal would proceed as smoothly as those in Saint John, and so they may have chosen the path of least resistance. In the spring of 2000 the last load of sugar cane from Cuba sailed into Saint John harbour for processing into various sugars. On July 28, 2000, the sugar refinery workers left their jobs for the last time.

Importantly, labour unrest is not really repressed as much as it is sublimated or channelled into other courses of action. Workers who feel locked in a struggle with employers for better wages and working conditions inevitably find informal methods of dealing with these issues. The suspension of the general strike gives way to countless acts of resistance and defiance inside the workplace. Tactics include more localized antagonisms with managers and supervisors, the application of "work to rule" strategies, maximum utilization of benefits and sick days, occasional product and machinery sabotage, "soldiering" (the slowing down of production wherever possible) and increased employee theft. Frustrated employees forced to accept concessions will express their grievances in creative ways. A strike-free workplace is not a happy, nor even a peaceful, workplace. Paradoxically, the precipitous decline in strikes across Atlantic Canada can go hand in hand with greater levels of dissatisfaction and frustration in the office or on the shop-floor.

Moreover, one must bear in mind that the strike option in Atlantic Canada has not withered. The decline of labour militancy should not be read as a sign that strikes are an anachronism in the new global economy. The labour truce in Atlantic Canada has been extracted under neoliberal economic duress; in a sense, workers are biding their time until a sustained economic upswing combines with rising public optimism about the economy to give them the confidence to "square the score" with employers. Then the years of roll-backs will themselves be rolled back. The incidence of strikes and lockouts in Atlantic Canada will rise, especially in those economic sectors—public administration, health care, natural resources and so forth—that are relatively stable and anchored to the region. Indeed, in the late spring of 2001 we may have seen a turning point in Atlantic Canadian labour relations. Throughout the preceding months healthcare workers in Halifax had been trying to reach a new contract with the Capital District Health Authority. During the difficult negotiations the government took the opportunity to introduce Bill 68, a law that would have taken away the right to strike from healthcare workers and have given the Cabinet the authority to impose contracts. On June 25 healthcare workers stopped work for a day of protest but immediately returned to work after the Nova Scotia Relations Board issued a cease and desist order. On June 27, workers from the healthcare bargaining unit (which is separate from the registered nurses bargaining unit) went out on a legal strike, and the government passed Bill 68 later on the same day. Facing heavy fines, registered nurses and healthcare workers decided to resign en masse. The government was forced to back down, especially since public sympathy was overwhelmingly on the side of the nurses and healthcare workers. The solidarity and determination of Nova Scotia's healthcare workers and nurses may have been a turning point in recent labour relations in Atlantic Canada, and it certainly drew a lot of attention across the region. A new compact between the gatekeepers of capital and the working people of Atlantic Canada will not emerge from any particular conflict or strike, but rather from the cumulative effects of many confrontations over a period of decades. Nevertheless, as these relations evolve, some events will prove to be far more decisive than others.

The Performance of Wages

The most likely implication of the sharp decline in the number of strikes and lockouts across the region will be stagnating real wages. To a considerable extent, this decline reflects the climate of austerity and the heightened sense of job vulnerability among labouring people, and it can thus be expected that organized workers have backed off from aggressively pressing their demands in the last two decades. Modest wage increases—even wages freezes and wage cuts—will be accepted reluctantly when the alternative prospects are believed to be long-term unemployment. With the cultivation of a recessionary psyche in the last two decades the sense of vulnerability will persist irrespective of the performance of the economy.

The data on major wage settlements measures the average annual percent increase in base rates (see Human Resources and Development Canada, Workplace Information Directorate 2001). A survey of major wage settlements in Atlantic Canada over the last two decades provides prima facie confirmation of our expectations regarding wage stagnation. Trends in Newfoundland and Labrador, Nova Scotia and Prince Edward Island in the 1990s were similar; major wage settlements exceeded the rate of inflation in those provinces about half of the time and, of course, fell below the rate of inflation in the remaining years. The exception was New Brunswick, where major wage settlements exceeded the rate of inflation seven times during the 1990s. Major wage settlements, moreover, tended to be erratic with respect to the rate of inflation and showed little responsiveness to levels of overall economic growth. The exception was Prince Edward Island, where major wage settlements exceeded the provincial rate of inflation in six straight years beginning in 1985, only to fall below the rate of inflation five out of six times between 1991 and 1996. In Nova Scotia, major wage settlements fell below the rate of inflation four years in a row beginning in 1994, and a similarly weak performance of major settlements appeared in Newfoundland and Labrador between 1992 and 1995. From this survey it could be expected that real wages have stagnated in Newfoundland and Labrador, Nova Scotia and Prince Edward Island and that they may have risen slightly in New Brunswick during the 1990s.

The analysis of wages in Newfoundland and Labrador shows that wages have not been keeping pace with the rate of inflation. For many wage earners in Newfoundland and Labrador, actual average week wages rose from $531.69 in 1992 to $587.64 in 2001, but these higher nominal wages failed to keep pace with the rate of inflation (Canada, Statistics Canada, *CANSIM II*). Figure 2.7 depicts the performance of average weekly wages in constant 1992 dollars. Between 1992 and 2001 real wages in Newfoundland and Labrador fell from $531.69 to $513.22, a loss of 3.5 percent. At one point, real wages had declined by more than 5 percent, but they recovered slightly in the last four years of our survey period. From 1993 to 1997 real wages were down from a high point of $535.17 to $504.53, a drop of almost 6 percent. It is clear that wages in Newfoundland and Labrador were struggling to hold their own against very low rates of inflation throughout the 1990s. The most optimistic interpretation of Figure 2.7 is that undulations in real wages are inevitable and that any ground lost to inflation can be made up relatively quickly, although there is no sign of this in the data. A less optimistic interpretation of Figure 2.7 contends that wage increases are clearly not keeping up with the rate of inflation and that we may be witnessing the front end of a historic wage decline anticipated by our reflections on the rudimentary social and political character of the new global order.

Figure 2.7
Real Wages in Newfoundland and Labrador

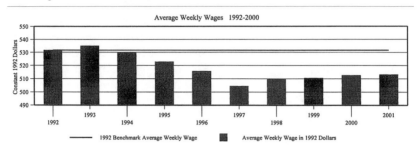

Source: Adapted from Canada, Statistics Canada, CANSIM II

Figure 2.8
Real Wages in Goods-producing and Service-producing Sectors

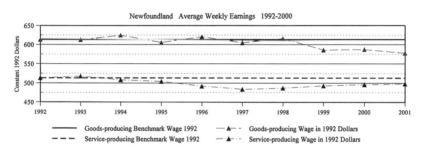

Source: Adapted from Canada, Statistics Canada, CANSIM II

A closer examination of real-wage performance in both the goods-producing and the service-producing sectors of the economy in Newfoundland and Labrador does not brighten the picture. Wage declines appeared in both sectors. As depicted in Figure 2.8, goods-producing wages oscillated around the 1992 benchmark wage for much of the 1990s but then fell off in the last three years of the survey period. The overall decline from a high in 1994 of $624.28 to a low in 2001 of $577.68 represented a deterioration of more than 7 percent of the value of the real wages in the goods sector. The real-wage decline over the full span of our decade-long survey period was 5.8 percent. In contrast to the goods-producing sector, real-wage declines in the service-producing sector were more or less steady until 1997, but a slight upturn was evident between 1998 and 2000. In the end, real wages in the service-producing sector declined from $512.95 in 1992 to $497.80 in 2001, a loss of 3 percent in value. It is important to note that only one in five workers in Newfoundland and Labrador work in the goods-producing economy, the sector that

Figure 2.9
Real Wages in Nova Scotia

Source: Adapted from Canada, Statistics Canada, CANSIM II

experienced the greatest declines in real wages. Nevertheless, seven out of every ten workers in Newfoundland and Labrador was employed in the service-producing economy in 2000, and real wages in this sector declined by 3 percent over the course of the survey period.

Real-wage declines in the region's largest economic jurisdiction were considerable in the decade between 1992 and 2001. Even the low rate of inflation in Nova Scotia during the 1990s could not prevent the drop. Although nominal or actual historical wages did rise from $515.47 in 1992 to $553.31 in 2001, by the end of the survey period real wages, expressed in constant 1992 dollars, stood at just $475.76. As Figure 2.9 shows, the decline was steady over the course of the decade and amounted to a loss of 7.7 percent in value. The conclusion that real wages in Nova Scotia have been performing very poorly in recent years is inescapable. There is no sign that the trend is about to be reversed in the near future. Over the longer term, it is inevitable that the revised class compact in Atlantic Canada will settle with respect to wages, but the point at which that will occur cannot be foretold with any greater degree of exactitude. The downward trends that we have seen in the last decade might be reversed, but wages could just as easily tail off more in years to come.

A closer examination reveals that the worst wage performance in Nova Scotia was in the service-producing sector, which employs two out of every three workers in the province. As depicted in Figure 2.10, between 1992 and 2001 real wages in the service sector declined from $501.62 to $457.20. This represents a steep loss in value of 8.9 percent in just ten years. Declines in the goods-producing sector of the economy were less. Between 1992 and 2001 real wages declined in the goods sector from $570.85 to $556.88, a value loss of 2.4 percent. Over the course of the decade real wages undulated around the 1992 baseline and then fell off in the last three years of the survey period. It is notable that real wages declined in both sectors of the economy in Nova Scotia between 1992 and

Figure 2.10
Real Wages in Goods-producing and Service-producing Sectors

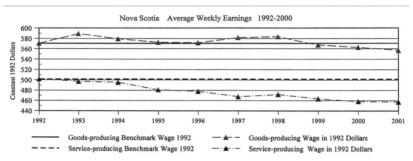

Source: Adapted from Canada, Statistics Canada, CANSIM II

Figure 2.11
Real Wages in Prince Edward Island

Source: Adapted from Canada, Statistics Canada, CANSIM II

2001 but that the sharper declines were in the much larger service sector.

As Figure 2.11 indicates, real wages also declined in Prince Edward Island from 1992 to 2001. During the middle part of the 1990s, however, owing undoubtedly to the construction of the Confederation Bridge, real wages performed reasonably well, and between 1992 and 1997 they increased from $467.62 to $481.81. Between 1997 and 2001, however, real wages on the island fell steadily, losing 7.7 percent of their value in just five years. Indeed, in 1998 and again in 1999, actual historical wages fell even before we factor the province's rate of inflation into the picture. Over the course of the entire survey period real wages on the island lost 4.9 percent of their value. It is clear that the construction of the fixed link between New Brunswick and Prince Edward Island boosted wages on the island, but it is equally clear that real wages have been in a tailspin since the project was concluded.

Figure 2.12
Real Wages in Goods-producing and Service-producing Sectors

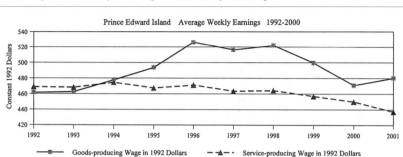

Source: Adapted from Canada, Statistics Canada, CANSIM II

The poor performance of wages in Prince Edward Island is evident when the goods-producing sector is examined apart from the service-producing sector. As we might expect, real wages in the goods-producing sector of the economy increased markedly while the bridge was being constructed, as evidenced in Figure 2.12. Between 1992 and 1998, real wages in the goods sector rose from $461.51 to $522.13, an increase of more than 10 percent in just six years. However, wages in the goods sector performed much more poorly between 1998 and 2001, and by the end of the survey period they had dropped back to $480.31. Still, over the entire course of the survey period real wages in the goods-producing sector of Prince Edward Island's economy rose by 4.1 percent. However, the goods sector accounts for less than 20 percent of the employment in the provincial economy. Figure 2.12 shows that wages in the much larger service-producing sector of the economy, the sector accounting for almost two-thirds of the jobs on the island, stagnated while the fixed link was being constructed and then began to tail off sharply after 1998. By the end of the survey period real wages in the service sector in Prince Edward Island fell by 6.7 percent.

The performance of wages in New Brunswick was the strongest in the region, although they fell slightly over the course of the ten-year survey period. As shown in Figure 2.13, real wages tended to undulate around the 1992 benchmark. Near the end of the 1990s they appeared to be falling off, but wages rebounded in 2000. Unlike the rest of Atlantic Canada, it cannot be said that real wages fell appreciably over the last decade. More importantly, however, it also cannot be said that they were on the rise.

The relatively strong performance of the service sector in New Brunswick undoubtedly figures prominently in the fact that wages tended to hold their own against inflation over the last decade. Unlike the rest of the

Figure 2.13
Real Wages in New Brunswick

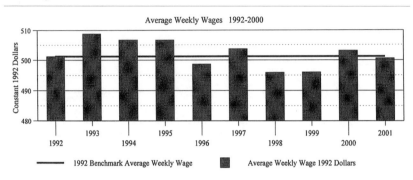

Source: Adapted from Canada, Statistics Canada, CANSIM II

Figure 2.14
Real Wages in Goods-producing and Service-producing Sectors

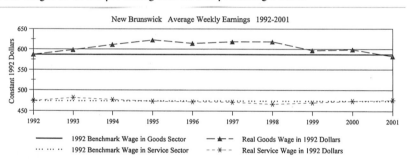

Source: Adapted from Canada, Statistics Canada, CANSIM II

region, real wages in New Brunswick's service-producing sector rose slightly between 1992 and 2001. As is clear from Figure 2.14, real wages in the service sector kept pace with the rate of inflation for the entire survey period. Although the overall gain of 0.4 percent is small, it stands out against the service sector declines of 3 percent in Newfoundland and Labrador, 6.7 percent in Prince Edward Island and 8.8 percent in Nova Scotia. Stronger wage performances in New Brunswick's service sector must be attributable, in part, to the lingering effects of the 1992 strike of public sector workers, a strike that signalled to the McKenna government that the well-being of public sector workers was not about to be compromised by government's embracing of neoliberal development strategies. It must also be added, however, that wages in the goods-producing sector of the New Brunswick economy performed well over the survey period. Of course, fluctuations in any given year are more easily attributable to the push and pull of large-scale economic development projects, including the Sable Island natural gas trunk and the construction of the four-lane Trans-Canada Highway between Fredericton and Moncton. In the end, the performance of wages in New Brunswick between 1992 and 2001 were the strongest in Atlantic Canada.

Atrophy of Labour Laws

Labour laws are paradoxical in numerous ways. They arise out of the spontaneous resistance of the working class, and then lock workers into formal procedures and legal routines that leave very little room for worker spontaneity and creative resistance. They emerge out of the collective power of the working class, but then necessarily establish standards that treat workplaces and workers as distinct entities. By partially shielding workers from the autocracy and abusiveness of managers and owners, labour laws represent historic achievements for the working class that, when established, undermine any further evolution in the class struggle against capital. In other words, labour laws are the product of class consciousness, but once they are operative they militate against the elevation of a collective consciousness among working people. Craig Heron's reflections on the impact of labour laws in the context of strikes in Canada early in the twentieth century are helpful to bear in mind:

> Stopping work illegally [in that time period] became known as a "wildcat" strike, and union officers became the "policemen" responsible for preventing such incidents. Sympathy strikes were clearly out of the question. The eagerness of Canadian workers to support each other's struggles, which had been evident for decades, had to be curtailed. Unless all contracts could be made to expire at the same time the Winnipeg General Strike could never happen again. Probably nothing would so effectively limit class consciousness among Canadian workers over the next forty years. (1989: 89)

Labour laws effectively channel the class struggle into tribunals and courts, the natural allies of capital insofar as these institutions deaden the class struggle. More particularly, labour laws offer some protection for workers, but they also create new avenues of legal retribution and punishment. On the whole they are a good thing; on the whole, they are also a bad thing. And when it comes to the matter of solidarity and collective consciousness, some labour laws are better than others.

Labour laws might very well stunt the development of working-class consciousness writ large, but they can still assist in the development of collective worker power inside the workplace or among a group of workplaces. That is, some laws help working people stand shoulder to shoulder against the abuses of particular firms or industries. Strong anti-scab legislation, for example, can give workers invaluable leverage against their employers. Similarly, laws easing the organization of a workplace can help workers form unions to resist the predations of their employers or to acquire some control over the office or shop-floor. Once again, laws that force employers to negotiate with newly formed unions—sometimes called "first contract" laws—foster the sense that collective action among working people can be fruitful and worth the struggle. These various laws can enhance the feelings of solidarity among working people, both by raising their sense of shared struggle in the context of the wage labour economy and by augmenting their power within the workplace.

When assessed in terms of their capacity to foster collective resistance inside the workplace, labour laws in Atlantic Canada are weak relative to those in the rest of the country. Moreover, in the era of globalization, any improvements in Atlantic Canada that could enhance the collective power of workers have not been legislated. Other jurisdictions, such as Ontario, have seen significant roll-backs in labour laws in recent years. In Atlantic Canada, where the labour laws are weak to begin with, especially those pertaining to the collective capacities of workers, doing nothing is doing a lot. Governments have simply held the line on labour law reforms—they had nothing to roll back. By failing to improve labour laws in Atlantic Canada in the last two decades, governments have gone a long way to maintaining a "business-friendly" investment climate across the region.

To elaborate, in the fall of 1994 the four labour federations from Atlantic Canada joined forces to call for an overhaul of regional labour laws. The campaign arose because of the perceived power of the business lobby in the region, the neoliberal outlook of many regional governments and the fact that labour laws in Atlantic Canada were weak compared with those of central and western provinces. In the climate of the early 1990s the federations of labour believed that there was "every likelihood that the four Atlantic governments will act in concert to undermine labour law" (New Brunswick et al. Federations of Labour 1994: 1.1). They argued that improvements in these areas were necessary since governments across the region embraced "the theory that poor labour laws are attractive to investors" (New Brunswick et al. Federations of Labour 1994: 1.1). Their efforts were known as the *Make It Fair* campaign, which included the dissemination of information to the public, education and feedback from the rank and file as well as the lobbying of legislators in each province.

Many of the explicit goals of the *Make It Fair* campaign pertained directly to the collective capacities of workers, especially their ability to negotiate with their employers from a position of dignity and strength.

For example, the labour federations promoted laws that would make it easier to organize the workplace. Their working document argued that "certification procedures often fail to promote and encourage free collective bargaining but provide obstacles to achieving it" (New Brunswick et al. Federations of Labour 1994: 2.4). The circular also observed that the certification process in each province involves "extraordinary delays" in the formation of a unionized workplace. "In many ways," the document argued, "these certification procedures have become an opportunity for employers to prevent collective bargaining by a variety of methods which frustrate the wishes of workers to be represented by a union in dealing with their employer" (New Brunswick et al. Federations of Labour 1994: 2.5; see also pgs. 1.4–1.8). Once the majority of workers are inclined to join a union, any delays favour the employers by giving them time to influence the attitudes of workers. Indeed, the province of Nova Scotia in 1977 was the first in Canada to add a second round to the certification process, that is, to require a certification vote once the requisite number of union cards were signed in any given workplace. Labour boards in the region, moreover, are sometimes given to attacks of officiousness and have, on occasion, killed a certification process on technicalities—trivial matters concerning the dotting of "i"s and the crossing of "t"s. As one might anticipate given the general social and political character of globalization, over the last two decades in Atlantic Canada there were no significant improvements in the laws pertaining to the certification process, a problem that is generally believed to be most glaring in Prince Edward Island.

A second change in labour laws called for by the *Make It Fair* campaign concerns the negotiation of a first collective agreement with a newly formed union. This law addresses the practice of employers to sometimes obstruct the negotiation of a first contract with a new union, interminably dragging out the process and wearing down the workers. First-contract legislation would address this problem by compelling the employer to reach an agreement. As the Atlantic Canadian federations of labour summarized in their 1994 campaign: "Even the best method of certification of trade unions will not vindicate the workers' right to organize if the employer decides to drag out collective bargaining so long that the wishes of the employees in organizing are frustrated" (New Brunswick et al. Federations of Labour 1994: 2.13; see also pgs. 3.13–3.15). Two provinces, New Brunswick and Nova Scotia, lack first-contract legislation altogether, and Newfoundland and Labrador and Prince Edward Island have only limited provisions pertaining to the imposition of a first contract. The 1994 amendments to Prince Edward Island's *Labour Act* included clear provisions for first-contract protocols. In the words of the Act:

> Where a trade union certified as bargaining agent and an employer have been engaged in collective bargaining to conclude their first collective agreement and have failed to do so ... the Minister may, upon request of either party, refer the matter to the board to settle the terms and conditions of the first contract.... The terms and conditions shall be issued in the form of a board order and shall be in effect ... for a period to be determined by the Board but not less than one year from the date of the order. (Prince Edward Island Legislative Assembly 1994: 213–14)

Unfortunately, although the amendments were passed, the section pertaining to first-contract legislation was never proclaimed. Had it been, the island would have been the first province in the region to have strong first-contract laws. Eight years after the *Make It Fair* campaign was launched, none of the Atlantic Canadian provinces have meaningful first-contract provisions.

A third important goal of the *Make It Fair* campaign pertained to anti-scab legislation. The capacity of workers to strike has been critical in the development of labour relations over the history of capitalism. At one time, when workers were highly skilled, they could not be so easily replaced when their labour power was withheld from an employer. Now, after decades of Taylorist refinements to the workplace and technological innovations to the labour process, the replacement of striking workers has become much easier. Labour laws, however, have failed to keep pace with these changing realities. At the time when anti-scab laws are most needed from the perspective of workers who seek leverage against their employers, few jurisdictions anywhere in the world have them. This is certainly the case in Atlantic Canada. Simply put, scabs are legal across the region, and it is very easy to deploy them on the modern shop-floor. In the last two decades there has been only one strong move in the direction of anti-scab legislation—the hearings on anti-scab legislation held by the Law Amendments Committee in New Brunswick in 1995. Although the law did not survive the third reading, it created the impression that the government of Frank McKenna was listening to working people across the province and that it might move to allow the passage of anti-scab legislation in the province. The fact that the government could permit public hearings on anti-scab legislation, however, strongly suggests that it could put the issue to sleep publicly while, in part, saving face with organized labour in the province. After listening to all "stakeholders" the government, not surprisingly, decided to kill the bill. Anti-scab legislation is the one law that immediately enhances the collective capacities of workers vis-à-vis their employers, and such a law had no chance of being passed in New Brunswick, just as it remains an unlikelihood throughout the rest of Atlantic Canada.

When it comes to strengthening worker resistance in the context of globalization, the last two decades have not seen any meaningful, across-the-board improvements to labour laws in Atlantic Canada. The collective capacities of workers in the region, at least from a legal standpoint, remain unchanged and generally are weaker when compared with the rest of Canada. A collectively strong work force with a strong sense of solidarity is altogether inconsistent with the buzz ideas about worker adaptability. In the Atlantic Provinces, ineffective labour laws and a fractionated working class greatly assist in capitalist "flexploitation."

The only improvements to labour laws in Atlantic Canada pertain directly to individually distinct workplaces and individual workers. Even in this aspect, however, developments have been uneven. Most of the region, for example, has been creeping towards "Sunday shopping," which directly harms workers by narrowing their free time. Similarly, improvements in expedited arbitration have been both modest and irregular, and many grievances can remain hung up in the legal system or the hearing process for far too long. Overall improvements to labour standards legislation have been modest. In 2000, for example, the government of New Brunswick amended its *Employment Standards Act*. Among other things, the amendments increased the minimum vacation of employees with eight or more years of continuous employment from two to three weeks. It also established that these long-term employees must be paid at least 6 percent of their wages one day or more before the vacation begins. Although such changes may have important consequences for individual employees, they are inconsequential in their general effect on worker solidarity. These are politically safe amendments that do nothing to change the balance of power between the leaders of business and working people across the region.

Conclusion

The consolidation of the new global order has not been particularly kind to established workers in Atlantic Canada. Rates of unionization across the region have stagnated, often at very low levels; labour militancy has bottomed out; real wages have stalled and, indeed, show signs of being on their way down; and labour laws have not been significantly improved anywhere in the region. The most optimistic assessment is that the Fordist labour regime in Atlantic Canada has been barely holding its own; it is perhaps fraying a bit around the edges but managing to afford Atlantic Canadians some protection against the autocracy of capital. A more pessimistic assessment is that we are witnessing the opening stages of a historic reversal in the fortunes of working people across the region. The Fordist class compact is in the process of being renegotiated, and the results of this process cannot be predicted with certainty. What is more than clear, however, is that an assault on the Atlantic Canadian working class has been afoot for the last two decades and shows no sign of abating in the near future.

Note

1. For a thorough review of Irving's union-busting strategies see Steuter and Martin 2000: 123–27.

Chapter 3

The Expansion of the Working Poor

In the spring of 2000 Prime Minister Jean Chrétien travelled to Sydney, Nova Scotia, to announce the opening of a new call centre. EDS Canada—formally known as Electronic Data Systems, a Texas-based company—had agreed to establish a call centre in the city's former K-Mart building. The "warm" or "inbound" call centre would receive calls from around the world and would employ about five hundred people to start. Over the next four years an additional four hundred employees were to be added to the company's payroll. The event was heralded by notable locals as an important step in the recovery of the struggling community. Nova Scotia Premier John Hamm expressed relief: "I have a great load on my shoulders. We are a financially-strapped province. But the load on my shoulders got a lot lighter today because of this announcement" (MacDonald 2000a: A1). Years of hardship and bad news were giving way to a more optimistic future anchored in the knowledge economy, which, according to the prime minister was establishing roots in Sydney: "Our government has taken a team Canada approach to making Canada a leader in the global-knowledge based economy. Today, EDS, the government of Canada and the government of Nova Scotia have shown the meaning of team work" (MacDonald 2000b: A1).

On the same day, news emerged that John Hamm's provincial government was cutting Sydney Steel's credit lifeline. Gordon Balser, the minister responsible for Sydney Steel, said that the decision to cut its credit lines was "in keeping with our commitment to end the day-to-day funding of Sysco's operations through taxpayer-funded lines of credit" (Government of Nova Scotia, Sydney Steel Corp. 2000). Over the next few months the Hamm government wrestled with the unpopularity of this decision in a region with chronically high unemployment. The decision proved fatal for Sydney Steel, and it would not take long before Sysco—the local appellation for the century-old steel-making company that employed hundreds of Cape Bretoners—would close its operations for good.

As the neoliberal faithful congregated in Sydney in March 2000 they painted an image of a bright and prosperous future for the struggling region. The economic changes afoot in Sydney corresponded with a familiar story about globalization, a story about the rise of the so-called new economy and the eclipse of the traditional economy. According to this story, the industrial pillars of the old economy—innumerable manufacturing facilities, resource-based enterprises, mining operations and heavy industries—must be restructured in the face of an increasingly competitive global economy. New industries rooted in technological innovation and the rapid circulation of ideas and information are on the rise. Local, provincial and federal politicians were in town to remind weary Cape Bretoners that they should be optimistic. The city and the region were coming "on-line" in the new "post-industrial age," creatively responding and adapting to new global realities. Or, as Prime Minister Chrétien rather blandly put it, Sydney was becoming "a leader in the global knowledge-based economy."

Such blithe reproductions of the rhetoric of the day do not capture the real meaning of developments in Sydney. To begin, the great global shift from a "hands-on" economy to an "ideas" economy has yet to transpire. Simple metalworking or metal-blending industries, including the manufacture of autos, steel, machine tools, aircraft and ships account for almost half of the largest five hundred corporations in the world. The characterization of globalization as a transition from an industrial economy to a cyber economy terribly overdraws the facts. An economy centred around the production and distribution of traditional goods and services, things that would have been familiar to our grandparents, has not withered. To be sure, it is spread out around the world more than it was even two decades ago, but the old economy continues to thrive and prosper.

Why this misplaced emphasis on the so-called new economy? What is the swollen rhetoric of globalization concealing? It is unlikely that we will ever hear a local politician say: "We endorse policies aimed at rolling your families out of $20-per-hour jobs and into $9-per-hour jobs. That is our goal. You older folks may have enjoyed respectable, high-paying jobs with decent benefits and long-term security in the past, but we would like to see your children working in non-unionized, low-paying jobs. So be patient, these things are for a greater good, and they take time." If the political vanguard of globalization spoke truthfully about the general features of globalization, features which they author and champion, voters in Sydney would undoubtedly turf them out of office at the first opportunity. To punch through these illusory claims and make sense of Sydney we must shift our analytical focus away from the rise or fall of certain industries and towards the character of the neoliberal public policy framework. Atlantic Canadians understand all too well that some economic sectors will take a hit now and then and that the fate of any particular economic sector or publicly-supported enterprise is as political as anything else. Established industries decline because contemporary politicians, guided by a neoliberal public policy agenda that emphasizes debt reduction, privatization, government downsizing and, more generally, free market principles, remove the regimes of public finance that sustained them. Neoliberal policies, in their turn, are infused with the long-term disciplining logic of the wage struggle. This basket of policies has been masterminded by transnational capital, but it gives all businesses the upper hand in the ceaseless struggle with workers over wages. There is no inexorable force bearing down on cities or regions, although the political elite frequently make such a claim to minimize the fallout from controversial decisions that bring irreparable harm to people and communities.

Developments in Sydney directly map onto the general features of neoliberalism and globalization. The primary thrust of the neoliberal agenda is to attack the Fordist worker on one side and the non-Fordist, unprotected or marginalized worker on the other. This two-pronged assault recognizes that there are two kinds of working people throughout the North. Although struggles during the twentieth century yielded tangible gains for the entire working class, not all workers enjoyed secure, well-paying jobs. For every "good" job in a unionized and relatively stable sector of the economy there have always been a number of "bad" jobs in which working people struggle every day. The neoliberal agenda strives to insure that this ratio does not change in favour of the good jobs, and it has been relatively successful to date. Neoliberalism bites at the heels of the Fordist worker at every opportunity, weakening the collective capacities of working people who are unionized and thwarting unionization in the low-paying, non-Fordist sectors of the economy. Sydney epitomized the changing profile of working life in much of the North over the last three decades. Approximately nine hundred bad jobs were about to be created while hundreds of good jobs were being thrown into jeopardy. It is an all-too-familiar episode across Canada: politicians grease the gears that permit good jobs to be cashed in for bad jobs. The city and the region were one step closer to exchanging Fordist-type workers in the steel industry for unprotected workers in a call centre, thus swelling ranks of the working poor in Atlantic Canada.

The plight of the working poor is the concern of this chapter. With respect to income, the overall rate of pay among the working poor is typically within a few dollars of the minimum wage, and the prospect of the wage rising significantly over the course of employment is bad. Front-line workers in the service industry are sometimes forced to sacrifice even this meager income during the initial few days of "training." Inside the workplace the working poor often face unsanitary, unsafe or even toxic working conditions. Workers who struggle to enhance the safety of workplaces are often punished with reduced hours or dismissal. Chronic sexual harassment from employers, co-workers and customers is a fact of working life for many women in low-wage jobs. Hours can be long and irregular, and many workers are often expected to work evenings and weekends. Moreover, many workers, especially those in the food service industry, are expected to be available for work outside of their regularly scheduled hours. To prevent a status change to "full-time employee" with its corresponding wage increases, many working people are deliberately "part-timed," that is, periodically laid off or denied the necessary weekly hours to reach the full-time threshold. Petty supervisory harassment and interference is rampant in low-end workplaces. High-tech surveillance and monitoring—video recording, audio recording, task timing, spot inspections and so on—are used more and more by employers. Without the protections of unions, the capacity of workers to respond effectively to these workplace intrusions and abuses is limited.

The working poor fair no better outside the workplace. The challenge of meeting the basic necessities of life have become more and more difficult. Working people often put in longer hours at their undesirable jobs simply to make ends meet. The focus turns to merely "getting by" in any particular month, making it through the holidays and staying one step ahead of bills and creditors. Long-term planning is out of the question. RRSPs and RESPs are luxuries they cannot afford. For the working poor, life is a daily grind. It is a struggle just to pay the rent and purchase groceries. In 1998 the *Saint John Telegraph-Journal* reported on the growing use of food banks in Atlantic Canada, stressing that the working poor were using the food banks more frequently. A volunteer from the Open Hands food bank in Moncton described one working-poor couple whose child had taken ill: "The man and woman both work at minimum wage.... A sick child and the money was gone. It wasn't [just] a story—I saw the prescription receipts" (*Telegraph Journal* 1998: A1). A director at the Metro Food Bank in Halifax reiterated that working people are often forced to put money into medication and other pressing necessities instead of food: "You get a lot of people who all of a sudden have to pay for dentist bills, for prescriptions, for all kinds of things, using what little they might have and leaving nothing for food" (*Telegraph Journal* 1998: A1). For the working poor life can be bitterly unpleasant. Vulnerability and anxiety mark the rhythm of each day. Hard work and long hours offer no guarantee against hardship.

From the vantage point of those toiling for low wages in Atlantic Canada, most jobs have a paradoxical nature. However unpleasant and low-paying it may be, a job can provide modest financial relief for struggling families. Indeed, the loss of employment can quickly lead to personal financial disaster. Many working poor in Atlantic Canada endure their jobs—that's all—to avoid an even worse fate. Employment is not taken lightly by anyone. Indeed, polls show that the fear of job loss is greatest among Atlantic Canadians, as is the fear that one is also likely to remain unemployed longer in the Atlantic region (Gallup Canada 1999: 1–3). Many workers are grateful for jobs, and yet they recognize that the work may be undignified, abusive and demeaning. Needing work is hardly the same as liking it or feeling satisfied. A job can provide both relief and despair, and the working poor in Atlantic Canada understand this paradox very well.

Poverty among working people has intensified in the neoliberal era. This direct connection is evidenced by the rising profile of the wage struggle across Canada in the neoliberal era. It is now commonplace for the elite to publicly question wage levels. Politicians repeatedly attack workers with higher wages, especially workers in the civil service, and call incessantly for wage moderation. Governments impose wage freezes and collective bargaining restrictions. Employers shred contracts and engage in aggressive decertification drives. Although all of these wage issues affect the working poor, it is the legislated minimum wage that bears on them most directly and immediately. It is to this matter of the minimum wage in Atlantic Canada that our attention now turns.

The Minimum Wage and the Working Poor

The suppression of the social wage is not a by-product of globalization; it is its inner principle. A clear assessment of globalization must not labour under the delusion that wages will rise in the shorter term nor under the misunderstanding that the downward pressures on wage levels number among globalization's many drawbacks. The former notion is fancy; the latter is akin to suggesting that nuclear fusion is merely one of the sun's many attributes. Globalization is about redoubling efforts to drive down all wages. It should come as no surprise, therefore, that minimum wages throughout the North have risen in political profile. The minimum wage has always constituted an important wage floor, and the legislative recognition and protection of the minimum wage was an important gain for working people in the twentieth century. As globalization gathers momentum, however, this critical baseline wage has intensified as a site of struggle. The battle over the minimum wage is important because of its trendsetting character. It provides the standard for other low-wage jobs and countless enterprises throughout the economy, especially those that employ only a handful of workers. A recent study by the Canadian Council on Social Development summarizes the relationship well: "The level of the minimum wage is important not only to minimum-wage workers, but also to those whose wages are $2 to $3 above the minimum rate. By establishing the level of the bottom rung on the income ladder, the minimum wage greatly influences the levels of the next few rungs as well" (Schellenberg and Ross 1997: 41).

This represents only part of the story, however. In an era devoted to "wage moderation," the lowest possible wage acts as a benchmark for the entire economy and assists in the suppression of all wages. This is accomplished, in part, by the interpretation given to the very visible gulf between low-end and high-end wages. A cleavage is easily created between the working poor and those in higher-paying jobs, especially in the civil service. With so many workers struggling in the low-wage range, workers receiving a salary well above the minimum rates can be more easily discredited, even vilified, in popular commentary. A striking public sector worker would be harder to impugn if the minimum wage was $12 or $13 per hour. When benchmark wages are extremely low, the striking higher-wage workers are easily portrayed as greedy and merely "out for themselves." The job of a government worker or an auto worker appears luxurious when compared to that of someone struggling at $6 an hour. Considering the neoliberal program's basic goal of attacking workers protected by the Fordist labour regime—workers in unionized workplaces earning respectable wages and so on—then a marked gulf between low-end wages and higher wages serves its ideologues and apologists well. It erodes public sympathy for upper-end workers throughout the economy, especially those in the public sector, where there has been an intense campaign to discredit government workers. When the minimum wage is suppressed, the message of wage moderation can be pressed with greater credibility by those seeking to keep Canada "competitive" in the new era of globalization. The minimum wage becomes a critical wage standard for all wages and salaries.

In Canada there has been a proliferation of studies and pronouncements on the minimum wage. Much of the ideological fodder now emanates from business-funded think-tanks, which invariably decry the very idea of a legislated minimum wage and relentlessly attack any increases in the provincial minimum wage rates. The Fraser Institute in Vancouver has been leading the reactionary charge. The following is a summary of the most common argument against raising the minimum wage, that is, that it has a drag effect on job growth:

> Among economists, there is a substantial consensus about the impacts of minimum wage legislation. Most economists would argue that increases in the minimum wage reduce employment and raise unemployment rates of unskilled workers. Furthermore, economists tend to agree that increases in the minimum wage are likely to do more harm than good. In particular, the bulk of the empirical evidence suggests that minimum wage laws tend to harm the groups these laws are intended to help—the young, the working poor, and the unskilled. (Law 1999: Introduction)

The study lamented that politicians, nevertheless, continue both to raise the minimum wage for "political" reasons—that is, to score popularity points—and to ignore the irrefutable economic truths proffered by right-wing economic think-tanks:

> Policy makers and politicians, however, continue to find this evidence unconvincing. In Canada, many provincial governments have raised, or are considering raising, minimum wages in efforts to help the working poor.... Hence, it would appear that political, as opposed to economic, considerations dominate when it comes to public discussion of the desirability of minimum wage legislation. (Law 1999: Introduction)

A second concern sometimes expressed in these studies focuses on the bluntness of minimum wage hikes as a policy instrument to redistribute income. The Fraser Institute's study on the minimum wage, by emphasizing the claim that most minimum wage recipients are young and live at home, contended that increases in the minimum wage helps those who are already well-off. Indeed, in the media release announcing the release of its study on the minimum wage (Fraser Institute 1999), the institute flagged this weakness directly:

> The idea that high minimum wages are a form of income redistribution is simply incorrect. Because the majority of minimum wage earners are young and unskilled, but not necessarily poor (think of all the teenagers greeting you behind the counter at your local fast food restaurant), the effect of the minimum wage is instead, to transfer resources to those who are already relatively well off.

Atlantic Canadians have their own version of the business-funded, neoliberal think-tank. The Atlantic Institute for Market Studies (AIMS) started with seed money from the Donner Canadian Foundation, and over the years it has enjoyed the support of many leading corporations, including the Bank of Montreal, the Royal Bank of Canada, the Bank of Nova Scotia, the Toronto-Dominion Bank, McCain Foods, Baxter Foods, Imperial Oil, ScotiaMcLeod, Kimberly-Clark and Southam Incorporated. The temper of AIMS regarding the minimum wage is somewhat more sensitive than that of the Fraser Institute, although its standpoint can still be remarkably callous when it comes to the working poor in Atlantic Canada. Even slight rises in the minimum wage have been greeted with ridicule and scorn from AIMS. Such right-wing hullabaloo was evident, for example, when Nova Scotia Labour Minister Guy Brown announced an increase in the province's minimum wage to $5.50 per hour by February

1997. AIMS ungenerously accused the Nova Scotia government of pandering to the masses: "Minimum wage increases rarely help the working poor. But governments continue to attempt to score points by giving minimum wage earners a pay raise. The minimum wage rate should be left to the markets" (Lacey 1996). The similarity between its position and that of the Fraser Institute eventually becomes evident. AIMS contends that a jump in the minimum wage will hurt the working poor by creating fewer jobs:

> The proponents of a raised minimum wage say this is necessary in order to allow low income earners to keep up with the rate of inflation and reach an acceptable standard of living. But does this argument make sense economically? What is the effect of an increase in the minimum wage on the Atlantic economy and workers? (Lacey 1996)

An answer echoing the conventional concern about the contraction of jobs is immediately offered:

> Young people entering the work force and unskilled workers end up paying the bill in hardship for increases in the minimum wage. Some companies which depend on minimum wage labour, if they can't increase the price of their goods or services, will be forced to cut their work forces in order to offset increases in the minimum wage. Other companies simply go out of business, no longer providing employment to anyone. Fewer people working weakens the regional economy. More importantly, this reduces the job pool for those who need work the most: people entering the workforce, who need to build their work experience, and the unskilled for whom employment provides the best opportunity for skill upgrading. (Lacey 1996)

The article concludes with the customary plea to let the markets determine the minimum wage: "Deregulation of wages would mean more jobs, and fewer people collecting social assistance" (Lacey 1996).

A second response to the minimum wage rate was also evident in the AIMS commentary. It linked an attack on increases to the minimum wage with another concern favoured by the right—the need to cut income taxes. According to Don Cayo, a former head of AIMS, arguments for and against minimum wages both contain a kernel of truth. With respect to raising the minimum wage he notes:

> The Atlantic Provinces have the lowest minimum wage levels in Canada, some will say. And they'll point out that people can't live

on that ... you don't need a study—a moment's reflection will do—to show how hard it is for people at the low end of the wage spectrum to make ends meet. At the same time, however, others will argue that increasing the minimum wage—like increasing any cost of doing business—will hurt the economy more than it will help. It will worsen the plight of the working poor—or poor people who'd like to be working—by slowing job creation, fostering cutbacks in working hours and, potentially, even leading to layoffs.... On the other hand, the effect may be a little more subtle, but there is no question that economic activity suffers when costs go up. Sophisticated businesses have a fixed amount they're prepared to spend on wages, and that's it. They won't be bullied into spending more. And unsophisticated businesses— like the very small ones run by some very energetic young people I know—are already netting less than minimum wage to their owners who work 70, 80 or 90 hours a week. Simply put, people like this have limits to how much more they'll pay their employees than they pay themselves. (Cayo 1999)

He concludes by stressing that the solution most advantageous to the working poor should focus not on the minimum wage rate but on lowering the taxes for low-wage workers:

If it's wrong to raise the minimum wage and slow job creation, and if it's wrong to leave working poor people with insufficient money to get by, why not just let them keep what they earn? Why not change the tax system to stop taking money from people who don't have any? (Cayo 1999)

There is nothing unique in the AIMS commentary on the minimum wage. The most obvious solution to the issue of the working poor, that is, increased wages, is rejected in favour of solutions that emphasize job creation and economic growth. These business-supported groups have resurrected antiquated and thoroughly discredited liberal notions of the labour market that rest on the fiction that an individual worker and an employer can simply come to an agreement about wages and working conditions. Wage ranges, they imply, will be determined by the overall balance between the supply of labourers on the one hand and the demand for workers on the other. History has proven, however, that the determination of wages is only vaguely related to supply of labour and demand for labour. It is the blunter collision of class power in society that governs wage levels. And, in this, the leaders of business will always have the upper hand because "the capitalist can live longer without the worker than can the worker without the capitalist" (Marx 1964: 65). A well-organized, militant work force is bound to drive up wages just as surely as a poorly organized and misled working class is bound to see its wages fall.

Utilitarian arguments against the minimum wage emanating from the intellectual guardians of the business community is the most telling instance of the commonplace outlook that overall economic health is more important than individual well-being. "Where the nation is rich its people are poor" was the more critical refrain bandied around in the past. An analyst with an eye to the ideological content of truth claims and a sensitivity to human hardship would immediately pose these questions: Is it better to have more low-paying jobs or fewer high-paying jobs, assuming, of course, that these are the only two options? Should we consider compensating the unemployed with reasonable levels of social assistance to keep the overall income levels up, assuming again that our only options are those so starkly presented by AIMS and other business-funded institutes? Are these really our only options? Could a rise in the minimum wage, for example, stimulate economic growth, as some writers have suggested? Even if we cut out all taxes for the working poor, what should we do about the fact that their gross wages would still be far below the poverty line? Should cutting taxes be the only option considered to help the working poor? Perhaps the promotion of a more progressive income tax, increases in the minimum wage and more generous income assistance programs would help the working poor? Should governments take on greater responsibility to help everyone who is struggling?

These straightforward, first-order questions are bound to arise in the context of reflective discussions about appropriate minimum wage levels, especially when the expansion of the working poor is so abundantly evident. Questions of this nature, however, are never seriously broached by AIMS or other business-friendly think-tanks. Although they claim an objectivity rooted in the "science" of economics, one could be forgiven for concluding that the singular goal of AIMS is to devise arguments that support free market principles. The Atlantic Canadian Institute is a tireless champion of neoliberal public policies. It chastises governments that deviate from a headlong commitment to free marketism, and its conclusions never stray far from the blunt promotion of unfettered capitalist activity in the region.

From the perspective of critical political economy the arguments of AIMS are not at all engaging, and they preclude a set of second-order questions regarding the character of society and the nature of public policy discourse. However, its political function cannot be overlooked, and it must be regarded as part of a generalized collection of political pressures that have been brought to bear on the issue of the minimum wage in Atlantic Canada. As this discussion will demonstrate below, the minimum wage over the last twenty-five years has been heading downwards, and some of the responsibility for this must be assigned to organizations, such as AIMS, that rationalize and defend neoliberal policies. The neoliberal ideologues have done their job. They might even be accused of overkill. Although it is understandable that the minimum wage is a site of struggle in the neoliberal era, the continuing focus upon it by the apologists of globalization is striking given the fact that it has fallen so precipitously in recent years. In a sense, working people in Atlantic Canada have already lost round one when it comes to the minimum wage. The relentlessness of AIMS and others can only be driven by their fear that the minimum wage might recover a bit in the future. Indeed, in the winter of 2002 the Hamm government, through its website, directly asked Nova Scotians if the minimum wage should be higher or lower or remain the same, a transparent exercise in democracy designed to insure the continued decline of the minimum wage in the province.[1] In a sense, the ongoing profile of the minimum wage reminds everyone of the adage that class struggle never takes its day of rest.

The history of the plunge of the minimum wage in the last twenty-five years is essential to understanding the expansion of the working poor in Atlantic Canada. Table 3.1 proves that at first glance, the minimum wage appears to have risen substantially in all four Atlantic provinces in recent decades. Indeed it more than doubled between 1976 and 2000. In Newfoundland and Labrador, it rose from $2.50 to $5.50, in Nova Scotia from $2.50 to $5.70, in Prince Edward Island from $2.50 to $5.60 and in New Brunswick from $2.80 to $5.75. The largest increase in the nominal minimal wage, therefore, was the 128 percent rise in Nova Scotia, while the smallest was 105 percent in the province of New Brunswick.

Table 3.1
Nominal Minimum Wage in Atlantic Canada[2]
1976–2000 Dollars

	1976	1980	1984	1988	1992	1996	2000	%Change
Newfoundland and Labrador	$2.50	$3.15	$3.75	$4.25	$4.75	$5.00	$5.50	120
Nova Scotia	$2.50	$3.00	$3.75	$4.00	$5.00	$5.35	$5.70	128
P.E.I.	$2.50	$3.00	$3.75	$4.25	$4.75	5.15	$5.60	124
New Brunswick	$2.80	$3.05	$3.80	$4.00	$5.00	$5.50	$5.75	105

Governments have proclaimed that such increases permit low-income earners to maintain purchasing power in their households. In 1996, for example, Nova Scotia Labour Minister Guy Brown heralded the increase in the minimum wage to $5.35 per hour as an important step to "help people keep pace with increases in the cost of living" (Government of Nova Scotia, Department of Labour 1996). To this supposed end, govern-

Figure 3.1
Falling Minimum Wage in Newfoundland and Labrador

Nominal and CPI-adjusted Minimum Wage 1976-2000

CPI-adjusted Minimum Wage ——— Nominal Minimum Wage — — —

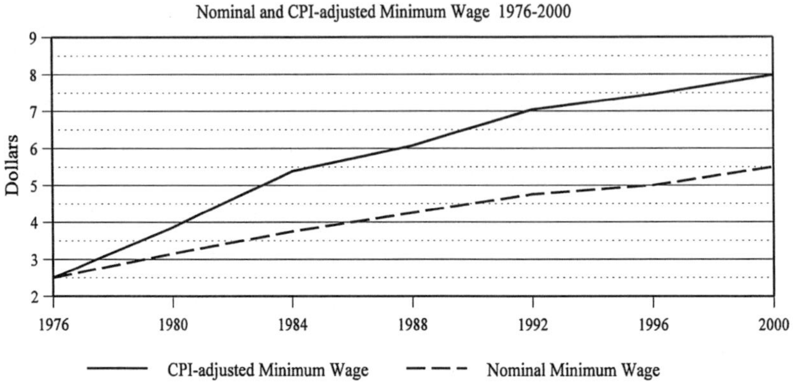

Source: Adapted from Canada, Statistics Canada, CANSIM II

ments in Atlantic Canada raised the minimum wage more than forty times over the last two decades—increases that have drawn fire from right-wing commentators and economic pundits, who generally contend that the labour market in Atlantic Canada is being distorted by government interference, which ultimately harms the working poor.

Increases in the minimum wage in Atlantic Canada have not been keeping pace with the rate of inflation, however. To demonstrate this we compare the legislated minimum wage in Atlantic Canada with the minimum wages adjusted to the inflation rates in each of the four provinces. Any differential against the Canadian Consumer Price Index (CPI)-adjusted minimum wage will provide an indication of the performance of legislated minimum wage at any point over the last twenty-five years. The substantial decline of the minimum wage in Newfoundland and Labrador is visually evident in Figure 3.1. Between 1976 and 2000 increases in the minimum wage failed to keep pace with the rate of inflation. By 1980, the CPI-adjusted minimum wage was $3.86 and the nominal minimum wage only $3.15, a difference of $0.71. By 1984 this gap had expanded to $1.63, and by the end of the decade it had reached more than $2. Finally, at the close of our survey period the CPI-adjusted minimum wage stood at $7.98, while the nominal minimum wage lagged behind at $5.50, a difference of $2.48. If the minimum wage in Newfoundland and Labrador had kept pace with the rate of inflation between the late 1970s and the close of the 1990s, it would have been almost $8 per hour. From the vantage point of the worker, the rate of $5.50 in 2000 was much worse that the rate of $2.50 in 1976. It is evident that the purchasing power of minimum wage work in 2000 is not comparable to the purchasing power of minimum wage work in 1976.

Figure 3.2
Falling Minimum Wage in Nova Scotia

Source: Adapted from Canada, Statistics Canada, CANSIM II

The minimum wage fared only slightly better in Nova Scotia between 1976 and 2000. As evident in Figure 3.2, had the minimum wage in the province kept pace with the rate of inflation over the survey period it would have stood at $7.97 in 2000; however, the legislated minimum wage was only $5.70, a gap of $2.27. This gap widened most dramatically between the mid-1970s and the close of the 1980s. By 1983, the legislated minimum wage had fallen behind the CPI-adjusted wage by more than $1, and by 1990 it lagged by more than $2. During the low-inflation periods of the 1990s the gap still expanded by more than $0.20. By the close of the survey period the minimum wage had fallen behind the pace of inflation by almost 30 percent. An hour of minimum wage work in 2000 simply did not go as far as an hour of minimum wage work in 1976. Although the minimum wage paid to employees in Nova Scotia more than doubled over the survey period, their purchasing power declined sharply.

A similarly poor performance is evident in Prince Edward Island. Although the nominal minimum wage on the island rose from $2.50 in 1976 to $5.60 in 2000, it was outstripped by the rate of inflation. A gap of more than $1 had opened up by 1983. By 1991 the gulf between the nominal minimum wage and the CPI-adjusted wage grew to more than $2. The minimum wage was spared by the low inflation rate in Prince Edward Island in the 1990s, a decade that saw two deflationary years in 1994 and 1998. The gap between the minimum wage and the CPI-adjusted wage of $2.37 in 1995 narrowed, owing to the incremental increases in the legislated minimum wage during the last half of the 1990s. At the close of the survey period the difference between the CPI-adjusted minimum wage and the legislated wage stood at $2.09. In other words, had the minimum wage kept pace with the rate of inflation on the island over the last two

Figure 3.3
Falling Minimum Wage in Prince Edward Island

Nominal and CPI-adjusted Minimum Wage 1976-2000

CPI-adjusted minimum wage   Nominal Minimum Wage

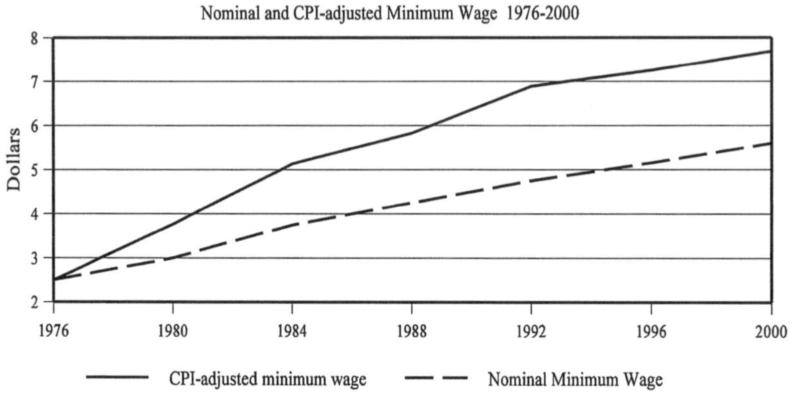

Source: Adapted from Canada, Statistics Canada, CANSIM II

decades, it would have been $7.69 instead of $5.60 in 2000. Figure 3.3 demonstrates that the income generated from minimum wage work in the mid-1970s in Prince Edward Island went a lot further than comparable work in the late 1990s.

The bleaker performance of New Brunswick's minimum wage over the same survey period is evident in Figure 3.4. In contrast to the other three provinces, the CPI-adjusted minimum wage in the province by the year 2000 was almost $9 ($8.84), and the corresponding gap between the minimum wage adjusted for inflation and the legislated minimum wage amounted to more than $3. This was the largest gap in the four Atlantic Canadian provinces at the conclusion of the survey period. As in the rest of Atlantic Canada, however, the minimum wage in New Brunswick tended to fare a little better in the low-inflation years of the 1990s. The largest growth in the gulf between the CPI-adjusted minimum wage and the nominal minimum wage occurred between the late 1970s and the mid-1980s, with a gap of more than $1 appearing by early 1979 and a gap of more than $2 appearing by 1985. Nevertheless, in 1995, just before the legislated increase in the minimum wage to $5.50 in 1996, the gap between the nominal minimum wage and the CPI-adjusted minimum wage had widened to more than $3.

A few observations regarding the performance of the minimum wage in Atlantic Canada can be made. First, nowhere in the region did the minimum wage keep pace with the rate of inflation. In all four provinces, the gap between the CPI-adjusted minimum wage and the nominal minimum wage was more than $2 by the end of the survey period. In New Brunswick, it was more than $3. The largest lags across the region were

Figure 3.4
Falling Minimum Wage in New Brunswick

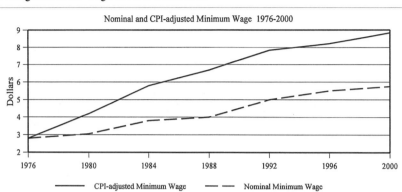

Nominal and CPI-adjusted Minimum Wage 1976-2000

——— CPI-adjusted Minimum Wage   — — Nominal Minimum Wage

Source: Adapted from Canada, Statistics Canada, CANSIM II

evident between the late 1970s and early 1980s. Nevertheless, the gap persisted throughout the low-inflation periods of the 1990s. In the end, not only did the legislated increases in the minimum wage fail to match the levels of inflation in all four provinces, there was not even a hint that the minimum wage rate might recover in the future.

The CPI-adjusted minimum wage provides a standard to assess the performance of the nominal or legislated minimum wage over a period of time. It can tell us what the minimum wage would have been in any given year, had increases in the wage been pegged to the rate of inflation in the mid-1970s in Atlantic Canada. In Nova Scotia, for example, the CPI-adjusted minimum wage passed the $5.60 mark in 1987, but the legislated minimum wage of $5.60 did not appear until 1999. Any survey based on the CPI-adjusted minimum wage, although revealing, is somewhat arbitrary insofar as the commencement date of the survey period is flexible. To minimize the effects of this discretion, this study has picked the widest possible time period, one that overlaps with the transition from Fordism to globalization and spans the high-inflation (early 1980s) and low-inflation (mid-1990s) years. Nevertheless, a less arbitrary measure of the performance of the minimum wage against the rate of inflation can be determined by calculating the real minimum wage. This permits us to speak with greater precision of the declining minimum wages across Atlantic Canada in the last twenty-five years.

In making more specific observations about the performance of the minimum wage in Atlantic Canada, we turn first to the province of Newfoundland and Labrador. Between 1976 and 2000 the real minimum wage, expressed in constant 1992 dollars, declined from $6.49 to $4.85. This represents a loss of more than 25 percent. Figure 3.5 depicts the

Figure 3.5
Real Minimum Wage in Newfoundland and Labrador

Source: Adapted from Canada, Statistics Canada, CANSIM II

Figure 3.6
Real Minimum Wage in Nova Scotia

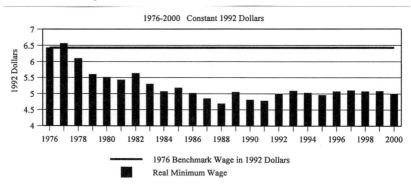

Source: Adapted from Canada, Statistics Canada, CANSIM II

gaps between the 1976 minimum wage and the real minimum wage from 1977 to 2000. The value of the real minimum wage fell more than $1 in value by 1982. The real minimum wage reached a low of $4.55 in 1995, a loss of almost 30 percent of its value, but recovered slightly in the latter part of the 1990s owing to three legislated increases in 1996, 1997 and 1999. These increases were not associated with substantial rises in the real minimum wage. Between 1986 and 2000 the real minimum wage in the province never rose above the $5 threshold. The best that can be said is that during the low-inflation period of the 1990s the real minimum wage held its ground against inflation but displayed no hint of recovering to its levels of the late 1970s and early 1980s. In short, the real minimum wage in Newfoundland and Labrador declined precipitously in the ear-

Figure 3.7
Real Minimum Wage in Prince Edward Island

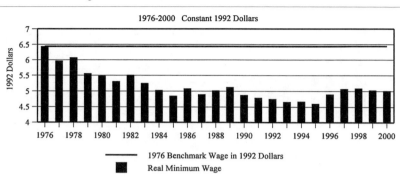

1976-2000   Constant 1992 Dollars

1976 Benchmark Wage in 1992 Dollars
Real Minimum Wage

Source: Adapted from Canada, Statistics Canada, CANSIM II

lier years and then stagnated through the latter years of the survey period.

The real minimum wage in Nova Scotia also declined substantially during the last twenty-five years. In 1976 it stood at $6.43. By 1981 it had lost one full dollar to inflation, and would continue its downward trend for most of the 1980s. By 1988 the real minimum wage in Nova Scotia had fallen to just $4.69, its lowest point in our survey period. Throughout the 1990s the real minimum wage in Nova Scotia hovered around $5. By the end of the survey period it had once again fallen below $5 for the sixth time in the last two and a half decades. Figure 3.6 illustrates the gulf between the 1976 benchmark wage of $6.43 and the declining minimum wage over the next two decades. Over the survey period, the minimum wage in Nova Scotia lost 22.6 percent of its value to inflation.

The real minimum wage in Prince Edward Island also evinced steep declines, especially in the late 1970s and early 1980s. As Figure 3.7 indicates, the real minimum wage fell quickly between 1976 and 1985, losing $1.59 or slightly more than 24 percent of its value expressed in constant 1992 dollars. Over the next few years the real minimum wage on the island fell even further, dipping past the $5 threshold in 1990 to a low of $4.60 in 1995. Indeed, for the first half of the 1990s, the real minimum wage in Prince Edward Island did not exceed $5. It was not until the legislated hike of 1997, a move that raised the nominal minimum wage from $5.15 to $5.40, that the value of Prince Edward Island's real minimum wage broke the $5 barrier. Nevertheless, in a little more than two decades the real minimum wage in Prince Edward Island fell from $6.44 (in 1976) to just $5.01 (in 2000). The overall decline of the real minimum wage was 22.2 percent. Again, the slight rise in the real value of the minimum wage was attributable to the increases of 1996 and 1997, but

Figure 3.8
Real Minimum Wage in New Brunswick

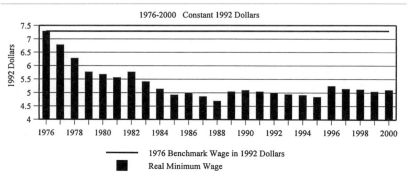

1976-2000   Constant 1992 Dollars

———— 1976 Benchmark Wage in 1992 Dollars

■ Real Minimum Wage

Source: Adapted from Canada, Statistics Canada, CANSIM II

there is little sign that the full value of the minimum wage will be restored in the near future.

The decline of the real minimum wage in New Brunswick since 1976 is staggering. At the opening of the survey period the minimum wage in 1992 dollars was $7.29. By 1988 the real minimum wage plummetted to $4.69. Figure 3.8 shows that over eleven years New Brunswick's real minimum wage lost 35.7 percent of its value. In the late 1980s and early 1990s the real minimum wage in the province gained back a fraction of its value. The pattern of a modest recovery in the real value of the minimum wage after a rate hike, followed by sustained decline until the next hike, is clearest in New Brunswick. By the end of the 1990s, the real minimum wage was only $5.10. Expressed in constant 1992 dollars, between 1976 and 2000 the real minimum wage declined by $2.19; this represents a loss of 30 percent of its value in a little more than two decades. For the last ten years the real minimum wage has stagnated around $5 per hour, and the prospect that it will recover some of its lost ground seems slim. The hourly wage for minimum wage workers in New Brunswick in 2000 yielded much less than that of their counterparts in the late 1970s.

Our examination of the real minimum wage in Atlantic Canada demonstrates that it has weakened considerably over the last two decades. Still, governments across the region boast that the minimum wage is keeping pace with the rate of inflation. In the mid-1990s, for example, Nova Scotia Labour Minister Manning MacDonald claimed that the legislated increase of the minimum wage to $5.50 was expressly designed to keep pace with inflation: "We are helping workers keep pace with the cost of running their households. We are helping them put a little more money in their pockets.... Nova Scotia has an excellent work force, and it's important that they're treated fairly" (Government of Nova Scotia,

Department of Labour 1997). Nowhere in the region has this been the case. The real minimum wage has fallen precipitously in all four Atlantic Canadian provinces, losing an average of 24.9 percent of its value across the region in a little more than two decades. Moreover, regional politicians stress that they are treating minimum wage workers fairly. In March 1999 when Newfoundland and Labrador's Minister of Environment and Labour Oliver Langdon announced an increase in the province's minimum wage he was unequivocal:

> This year the province will lead the country in economic growth and we want to share this success with low wage earners. I believe that a modest increase in the minimum wage is affordable without placing undue financial hardship on small businesses while easing the burden on low wage earners.... Government is committed to providing an adequate minimum wage for low income earners. (Government of Newfoundland and Labrador, Department of Environment and Labour 1999)

Prince Edward Island's Community Services minister spoke about a prospective hike in the minimum wage with even more empathy for the working poor: "Our government cares deeply about the wages of low income earners.... We are concerned about those with low incomes and are striving to give them more support" (Government of Prince Edward Island 1999).

Despite these claims, legislated minimum wage rates do not enhance the quality of life for Atlantic Canadians. The minimum wage is not a living wage anywhere in the region. It consigns working people to chronic hardship and struggle and robs them of their dignity. Indeed, as Table 3.2 reveals, the sharp decline in the value of the minimum wage means that even full-time work at minimum wage will not lift a single person above the poverty line anywhere in Atlantic Canada.

On average, in 2000, the single person fell short of meeting normal living requirements by a little more than $4000 dollars per year or about $333 each month. The annual poverty gap—the dollar gap expressed as a percentage of Statistics Canada's low-income cut-offs (LICOs)—for a single person working at minimum wage in the region averaged 25.5 percent. This means that minimum wage income for a single person in Atlantic Canada meets only about three-quarters of a person's normal living expenses. The greatest gap was in St. John's, where a single person would fall $4317 below the poverty line, producing a poverty gap of 27.4 percent. In each province the average monthly dollar gap is roughly equivalent to the cost of a bachelor apartment in its sample city. In fact, the monthly dollar gap exceeded the cost of a bachelor apartment in St. John's. This provides some insight into the burdens on minimum wage workers in

Table 3.2
Minimum Wage and the Poverty Gap in Atlantic Canada
Single Persons 2000

	St. John's	Halifax	Charlottetown	Saint John
Minimum Wage	$5.50	$5.70	$5.60	$5.75
Gross Annual Income	$11,440	$11,856	$11,648	$11,960
Low-income Cut-off (Poverty line)	$15, 757	$15,757	$15,648	$15,757
Dollar Gap	$4,317	$3,901	$4,000	$3,797
Poverty Gap	27.4 %	24.8 %	25.6 %	24.1 %
Monthly Dollar Gap	$359	$325	$333	$316
Cost of Bachelor Apartment	$344	$491	$371	$344

Source: Adapted from Canada, Statistics Canada, CANSIM II

Atlantic Canada. To "get by," and little else, a person working at the minimum wage must strategize to avoid many of the normal costs facing single people, and obvious solutions include living with friends or family to eliminate rental costs altogether.

Table 3.3 shows the minimum wage rate required for a person to live with dignity by working a conventional forty hours each week. In all four provinces, this required minimum wage rate was more than $7.50 per hour. In 2000, no Atlantic Canadian province was within $1.50 of this required rate. The legislated minimum wage in Newfoundland and Labrador was two full dollars shy of this required rate.

The poverty gap can be attributed to the declines in the minimum wage over the last twenty-five years. Table 3.3 shows that the CPI-adjusted minimum wage exceeds the LICO-adjusted minimum wage in each of the four cities. In every city the CPI-adjusted minimum wage would have been sufficient to lift a single wage-earner over the poverty line. In other words, had increases in the minimum wage kept pace with the rate of inflation over the last twenty-five years, then the minimum wage would have been sufficient to lift a single person above the poverty line anywhere in the region.

Our discussion of the minimum wage to this point has been based upon the best possible scenario. That is, it has assumed that a person working for minimum wage is not trying to support a family. We have demonstrated unequivocally that the minimum wage rates in Atlantic Canada cannot support a worker who is single and childless, let alone one who is struggling to raise children. It is notable that business-supported think-tanks and many economists trivialize the concern about the minimum wage by arguing that most minimum wage earners are very young and usually live at home. They justify low minimum wages with the claim

Table 3.3
Minimum Wage and Minimal Dignity in Atlantic Canada
Single Persons 2000

	St. John's	Halifax	Charlottetown	Saint John
Minimum Wage	$5.50	$5.70	$5.60	$5.75
Minimum wage required to meet LICO (LICO-adjusted minimum wage)	$7.58	$7.58	$7.52	$7.58
CPI-adjusted minimum wage	$7.98	$7.97	$7.69	$8.84
	+ $0.40	+ $0.39	+ $0.17	+ $1.26

Source: Adapted from Canada, Statistics Canada, CANSIM II

that "only a small fraction of people earning the minimum wage provide the sole support for a family" (Lacey 1996). According to a piece by the Atlantic Institute for Market Studies, for young, inexperienced workers "having a job can be more important than the rate of pay—it is their path to increased prosperity in the future" (Lacey 1996). Clearly, it is inappropriate to engage in such peculiar ethical arguments, arguments that have been so thoroughly discredited over the years. These positions rest on the shameless assumption that wages should be contingent upon the profiles of working people—age, sex, marital status and so on. This argument has been used to justify the suppression of women's wages for decades, and it is no more palatable with respect to younger people. Working people themselves are best positioned to determine their wage needs, and if wages were truly determined by liberal models of the so-called labour market, all wages would be much higher.

To further our analysis of the plight of the working poor in Atlantic Canada we must focus on the anchor effect of the minimum wage across the region. It is the function of the minimum wage as the baseline wage that renders it so important in the era of globalization when concerns about the social wage have become paramount. A very basic question must be posed: How many people work at an hourly wage rate that is close to the minimum wage?—or, somewhat facetiously: As people pass through minimum wage work on their way to "prosperity," do the vast majority of them land in high-wage jobs?

The Anchor Effect of the Minimum Wage in Atlantic Canada

Do most jobs gravitate away from the minimum wage? To what degree does the minimum wage function as the benchmark wage in Atlantic Canada? To determine the answer to these questions we have calculated the quartile wage levels across the region. These measures indicate the number of hourly-wage earners who fall above or below a specific wage. The median wage, for example, identifies the wage level that splits hourly-wage earners into two equal groups, with one half earning more than the median wage and the remaining half earning less than the median wage. For this study, median and lower quartile wages are examined in some detail. As our discussion will elaborate, a large number of workers in the Atlantic Canadian provinces work at wages close to the minimum wage, a fact that sheds light on the increasing profile of the working poor across the region.

We turn first to the matter of the median wage. Figures 3.9 and 3.10 demonstrate that the median wage in the Atlantic Canadian provinces varied by more than $1 in 2000. New Brunswick had the highest median wage at $12.45 per hour, and Prince Edward Island the lowest median wage at $11.40. The median wage in Newfoundland and Labrador was $12.02, and the median wage in Nova Scotia was exactly $12. The average median wage across the region was just under $12 per hour in 2000. This figure means that about one half of the hourly-wage earners in Atlantic Canada worked for $12 per hour or less—in other words, within about $6.50 of the minimum wage. The greatest difference was in New Brunswick, where the minimum wage/median wage differential was $6.70. The smallest difference of $5.80 was in Prince Edward Island. The gap in Newfoundland and Labrador was $6.50, and the gap in Nova Scotia was $6.30. It is important to stress that the median wage is the highest hourly wage achieved by half of the wage earners in Atlantic Canada. Even work at the median wage rate means that a family will be living from paycheque to paycheque. For example, an individual supporting a family of four on the median wage anywhere in Atlantic Canada will not be able to lift that family above the poverty line. In 2000, a worker's gross median wage in Halifax, for example, would have yielded about $25,000 over the course of a year. The low-income cut-off for a family of four, however, was $30,000 (adapted from Canada, Statistics Canada 2001). To rise above the poverty threshold the wage earner in the family would have been forced to work longer hours, or the second adult would have had to venture into the work force while trying to manage daycare and after-school care.

Of course, many wage earners on the lower side of the median wage will be working in the $9 to $10 per hour range across Atlantic Canada. Families with income earners in these wage ranges must resort to an endless series of strategies—flyer surfing and coupon clipping, the rotation of monthly utility payments, late payments on utilities, credit cards, cash advances, irregular servicing of automobiles, "low-shop" weeks for groceries, rental delays, daycare from family members, etc.—to lower monthly costs. Many of these families may not formally fall below the poverty line because of the long hours put in by the adult wage-earners. In St. John's, for example, two adults working at $10 per hour and trying to

Figure 3.9
Statistical Snapshots of the Working Poor #1
Atlantic Canada

Median and Lower Quartile Hourly Wages in Newfoundland
2000

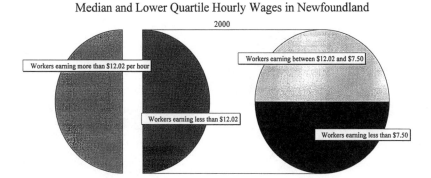

Median and Lower Quartile Hourly Wages in Nova Scotia
2000

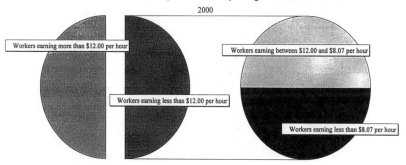

Source: Calculated from Canada, Statistics Canada 2001

support a family with three children must put in at least sixty-three hours of work each week to cross the poverty line, the equivalent of one full-time job and one half-time job, plus the challenges of child care (adapted from Canada, Statistics Canada 2001).

We get a better sense of the circumstances that arise when wages fall below the median wage when we observe the lowest income quartile in each of the Atlantic Canadian provinces. This measure identifies the wage level that splits the lower median wage workers exactly in half. As Figure 3.11 shows, at least half of the lower median wage workers cluster within about $2.50 of the minimum wage in all four Atlantic Canadian provinces. In Newfoundland and Labrador, for example, the gap between the minimum wage and the lower-quartile wage was exactly $2. That is, in the year 2000, 25 percent of all hourly-wage earners in the province were being paid between $5.50 per hour (the legislated minimum wage in 2000) and $7.50 per hour. In Nova Scotia the gap between the two wage

Figure 3.10
Statistical Snapshots of the Working Poor #2
Atlantic Canada

Median and Lower Quartile Hourly Wages in Prince Edward Island

2000

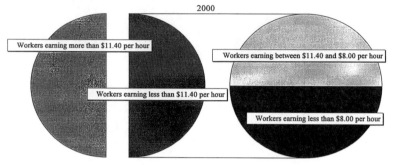

Median and Lower Quartile Hourly Wages in New Brunswick

2000

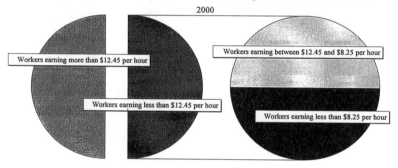

Source: Calculated from Canada, Statistics Canada 2001

markers was $2.37, and in Prince Edward Island the gap was just slightly higher at $2.40. The largest gap was in New Brunswick, where the lowest quartile of wage earner made between $5.75 per hour and $8.25 per hour, a difference of $2.50.

These numbers demonstrate the anchor effect of the minimum wage in Atlantic Canada. A large number of wage earners hover just above the minimum wage rate in each of the four provinces. The clustering effect for the lowest quartile of wage earners in the region is more evident when we note that the gap between the minimum wage and the lower quartile wage was invariably much lower than the gap between the lower quartile wage and the median wage across the region. In New Brunswick, for example, incomes among the lower quartile of workers ranged over $2.50 per hour, whereas incomes for the second quartile ranged over $4.20 per hour. In other words, the lowest quartile of wage workers were spread out over a much smaller income range, a range that clung to within $2.50 of

Figure 3.11
Anchor Effect of the Minimum Wage

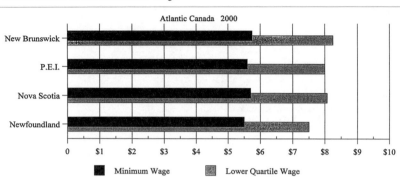

Source: Adapted from Canada, Statistics Canada, Labour Force Historical Review

the minimum wage in New Brunswick. In Newfoundland and Labrador, this clumping of the lower quartile of wage earners was even sharper, with the lowest quartile wage earner staying within $2 of the minimum wage, while the next quartile ranged over more that $4.50 per hour.

The data on quartile income provides some insight into the plight of the working poor in Atlantic Canada. It shows that a large number of wage earners tend to cluster in jobs with wages very close to the minimum wage. At least 25 percent of all wage earners across Atlantic Canada were within about $2.50 of the minimum wage in 2000. These findings are summarized in Figure 3.11.

At the other end of the wage spectrum, over half of the wage earners made more than $12 per hour across the region. At least 25 percent of all wage earners made more than $18.28 in Newfoundland and Labrador, $17.41 per hour in Nova Scotia, $16.00 per hour in Prince Edward Island and $18.03 in New Brunswick in 2000. Clearly, the opportunity to pass into high-wage work exists across the region, but barely half of the wage earners in any of the provinces enjoy earnings that provide them with comfortable levels of living. Also, the opportunity to slide into high-wage jobs is not a matter related to the normal cycle of adult life but rather to an individual's class and educational background. So many workers in Atlantic Canada remain stuck in bad jobs with very low wages, and this turns life into a terrible monthly grind.

As presented in Table 3.4, the lower quartile wage will not easily lift a family of four out of poverty anywhere in the region. In 2000, the highest poverty gap of 21.1 percent was in St. John's, while the lowest poverty gap of 13.2 percent was in Saint John. The estimated monthly dollar gap ranged from $326 in Saint John up to $521 in St. John's. Table 3.4 also presents the average cost of a two-bedroom apartment in each city to

Table 3.4
Lower Quartile Wage and the Poverty Gap in Atlantic Canada
Four-person Family 2000

	St. John's	Halifax	Charlottetown	Saint John
Lower Quartile Wage	$7.50	$8.07	$8.00	$8.25
Gross Annual Income (Based on 60 hours per week /1 full-time and 1 half-time job)	$23,400	$25,178	$24,960	$25,740
Low-income Cut-off (Poverty line)	$29,653	$29,653	$29,448	$29.653
Dollar Gap	$6,253	$4,475	$4,488	$3,913
Poverty Gap	21.1%	15.1%	15.2%	13.2%
Monthly Dollar Gap	$521	$373	$374	$326
Cost of Two-bedroom Apartment	$551	$649	$543	$460

Source: Adapted from Canada, Statistics Canada,
CANSIM II and Labour Force Historical Review

gauge the shortfall for a family of four with wage earners around the lower quartile mark. In St. John's, the monthly dollar gap was almost equivalent to the cost of a two-bedroom apartment. In Saint John, the monthly dollar gap was about two-thirds the cost of a two-bedroom apartment, and in Halifax the gap was a little more than half. As Table 3.4 shows, a family with wage earners hovering around the lower-quartile wage range will be struggling to rise above the poverty threshold.

The deepening exploitation of women in the South has been examined extensively in recent years. Women comprise most of the labour force in the world's two hundred or more zones of intensified manufacturing production. Within these factories they endure an appalling array of abuses, including sexual, verbal and physical assaults; repeated exposure to dangerous chemicals; repetitive strain injuries; intrusive surveillance procedures; no labour rights; and below-subsistence pay. The absorption of women into the super exploitative factories of the South was the product of an intense phase of export-oriented agriculture in the post-Second World War period, a phase known as the Green Revolution, which worsened community poverty and dislodged even more women from their land around the world. Outside the factories the lives of women are often torn apart by the decay and misery of communities riven by high poverty, chronic unemployment and generalized despair. Other women have been drawn into the folds of globalization in even more distressing ways. Many work as domestics for middle-class families in the world's cities. After travelling thousands of miles for desperately needed work, these women

Figure 3.12
Atlantic Canadian Women and Low Incomes 2000 #1

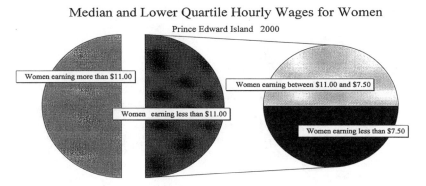

Median and Lower Quartile Hourly Wages for Women
Prince Edward Island   2000

Women earning more than $11.00

Women earning between $11.00 and $7.50

Women earning less than $11.00

Women earning less than $7.50

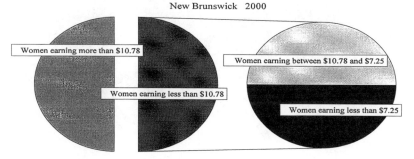

Median and Lower Quartile Hourly Wages for Women
New Brunswick   2000

Women earning more than $10.78

Women earning between $10.78 and $7.25

Women earning less than $10.78

Women earning less than $7.25

Source: Calculated from Canada, Statistics Canada 2001

often endure chronic mistreatment and low pay without the familiar comforts of their own culture and language. An even greater number of women work in the informal sectors of the global economy, as street vendors, seamstresses and clerks. The trials of this work have been widely observed, and they range from chronic harassment to withheld pay. Many women have entered the global sex trade, either forcibly or by dint of poverty. The global sex industry has been spurred on by the frequent movement of business executives, speculators and tourists in this era of globalization, and countless young women have been robbed of their lives and well-being as a result of the global sex regime.

As Figures 3.12 and 3.13 show, the quartile income data for Atlantic Canada also reveals that women disproportionately bear the burden of low-wage work across the region. The abuses of female workers in the North may not always be as dramatic as the superexploitation of women in the South, but the personal injuries, burdensome wages, chronic harassment and sustained abuses are still widespread. The differences in

Figure 3.13
Atlantic Canadian Women and Low Incomes 2000 #2

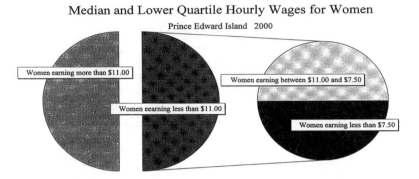

Median and Lower Quartile Hourly Wages for Women
Prince Edward Island   2000

Women earning more than $11.00

Women earning between $11.00 and $7.50

Women eearning less than $11.00

Women earning less than $7.50

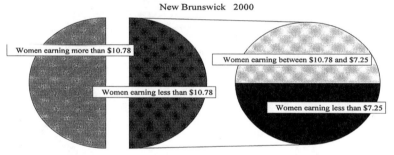

Median and Lower Quartile Hourly Wages for Women
New Brunswick   2000

Women earning more than $10.78

Women earning between $10.78 and $7.25

Women earning less than $10.78

Women earning less than $7.25

Source: Calculated from Canada, Statistics Canada 2001

quartile incomes for men and women in Atlantic Canada indicate that the lower quartile wages for women hover much closer to the minimum wage rates across the region. Figure 3.14 demonstrates that the difference in the quartile wage for males and females is striking in every province. In Newfoundland and Labrador, the lower quartile wage for men was $10.00 in 2000, but the same wage for women was just $6.07, a difference of $3.93. In Nova Scotia the lower quartile wage for women was $7.32 more than two dollars below the comparable wage of $9.50 for males. Prince Edward Island saw a difference of $1.00 between the two lower quartile wages in 2000, but this is attributable to the fact that the lower quartile wage for men was much lower when compared to the other three provinces. In New Brunswick, the lower quartile wage for women was $7.25 while that of their male counterparts was $10.00, a difference of $2.75.

These measures are important for at least two reasons. First, they show that males in the lower quartile range are more successful in pulling away from the minimum wage than their female counterparts. As summarized in Figure 3.14, the lower quartile wage for men was substantially

Figure 3.14
Anchor Effect of Minimum Wage for Men and Women

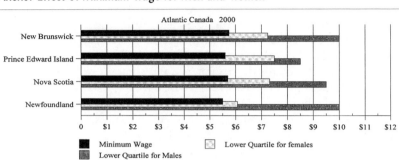

Source: Calculated from Canada, Statistics Canada 2001

higher than the minimum wage in every province. The greatest difference was in Newfoundland and Labrador, where the lower quartile wage for males was more than $4.50 above the minimum wage. In sharp contrast, the comparable difference for female workers in Newfoundland and Labrador in 2000 was a mere $0.57. New Brunswick recorded the next greatest gulf between the lower quartile wage for males and the minimum wage at $4.25, while the comparable gap for females in New Brunswick was $1.50. The differential anchor effect of the minimum wage for males and females is also very evident in Nova Scotia, where the lower quartile wage for men rose $3.80 above the legislated minimum wage, while the same measure for women was only $1.62. Only in Prince Edward Island was the gap noticeably closer, with the lower quartile wage for men at $2.90 in the year 2000, and the corresponding wage for women $2.00 above the minimum wage. Importantly, the closeness of the lower quartile wage levels for both men and women in Prince Edward Island speaks to the lower across-the-board wages on the island.

The differential wage data for men and women in Atlantic Canada is revealing. Analysis of the data shown in Figure 3.12, 3.13 and 3.14 reveals that in 2000 women comprised just slightly less than half of the work force across the region. However, the lower quartile wages for women suggest that about one quarter of all female workers received an income that is perilously close to the minimum wage. At least 25 percent of the female workers in Atlantic Canada were within about $2.00 of the minimum wage. A disproportionate number of women work at rates close to the minimum wage in all four Atlantic provinces. Moreover, the median hourly wage for women in each province was never more than $5.40 above the minimum wage, and in Newfoundland and Labrador this difference was just $4.56. In other words, half of hourly wages for women in Atlantic Canada were never greater than $11.00. The gendered nature of the minimum wage anchor is abundantly evident. It is not merely the case that the average wages of women are lower than those of their male counterparts, but rather that so many female workers throughout the region are working in the low-end, low-wage jobs.

The conclusion that women disproportionately bear the burden of low-wage work in Atlantic Canada is inescapable. In the past, many have consoled themselves with the argument that women's work is somehow less important than men's work. The fact that it is women who are disproportionately absorbed into the low-wage jobs can be explained only by the ever-present effects of patriarchal consciousness. In the South we know that women are drawn into the work force for a variety of reasons, including assumptions that they are more suited to dull, repetitive work, that their fingers are more "nimble," and that they are more docile (attitudes that would be readily voiced by factory managers), and because local managers desire to prey upon female workers sexually (an attitude that is never acknowledged). It is difficult to gauge the degree to which these factors are operative in the absorption of women into the low-wage work in Atlantic Canada. In can be reasonably supposed, however, that one argument routinely offered to justify low wages in the South, namely, that women's income is always supplementary to a man's income, is undoubtedly operating across the region. Over the years we have been treated to the persistent claim that men are the breadwinners and that women earn "pin money," that men bring in the family wage while women earn nothing but a supplementary family income. To many analysts these worn out arguments are immediately recognizable as attempts to justify the low wages paid to women. The belief, however, undoubtedly lingers. A manager of a tourist business in Cavendish or a retail clothing store in St. John's or a call centre in Moncton might very well be disposed to hiring more women by virtue of this prevailing cultural conviction.

Conclusion

In the fall of 1998 the Halifax *Chronicle-Herald* ran an article on social reform in Nova Scotia. In the article Pictou County Councillor Ed MacMaster spoke about the minimum wage: "There is probably enough work out there for everyone, but at $5.50 an hour there's no use going" (Graham 1998: A2). Such candour from a politician is uncommon. In this one remark this local politico draws links between the minimum wage, unemployment, low-wage work and poverty. Even more importantly, perhaps, he does so from the standpoint of the working poor and the unemployed. Unemployment persists, in part, simply because wages are too low in far too many jobs. Operators of restaurants and coffee shops regularly complain about their inability to get help. Working people know that low wages often do not go far enough. And when one factors in the bad hours, the child care problems, the workplace harassment and so forth, it just isn't worth it.

Nevertheless, more and more people find themselves in low-wage jobs across Atlantic Canada. The discussion in this chapter regarding minimum wage and low-wage work confirms the common impressions about working people who are struggling across the region. The quartile wage data in particular offers a statistical subtext to the growth of low-wage work anticipated in our discussions about the nature of globalization. Many wages in the region are not living wages. The minimum wage, for example, does not allow a single person—let alone a family —to rise above the poverty line. And the lower quartile wage in every Atlantic Canadian province fails to lift a family of four above the poverty line even if one adult works full-time and the other half-time—sixty hours per week on top of the management of child care. Worse still, it is apparent that a disproportionate number of low-wage jobs in Atlantic Canada are filled by women, a fact that brings the region into line with the rest of the world in a way that politicians and business leaders would be uncomfortable admitting.

As implied by the remarks of the local councillor from Pictou, Nova Scotia, the minimum wage, low-wage work, poverty and unemployment are intertwined. What was not acknowledged in MacMaster's comments, however, is the fact that the social assistance regime recognizes that working people routinely make these sort of calculations and accordingly gears its rates to force recipients into the work force, into the "bad" jobs with low wages. Unemployment certainly persists across the region, and it helps to keep wages depressed to a degree. It is the insufficiency of social assistance programs, however, that really insures that there will be a pool of low-wage workers. Atlantic Canadians are driven into low-wage work because the alternatives are even worse. We turn our attention to these dynamics in the next chapter.

High unemployment and mind-boggling poverty are facts of life in the era of globalization. It has been estimated that almost one billion people in the world are unemployed or underemployed and that about one billion people are also living in absolute poverty. In a world committed to driving down wages, it must be observed that high unemployment and extensive impoverishment contribute to this broad goal. As we will see in the next chapter, the same holds true in Atlantic Canada. The rising rates of poverty and persistent unemployment that rightly disturb so many caring people across the region has a wage dividend that makes it tolerable—and then some—for many elites.

Notes

1. Government of Nova Scotia, Department of Labour. 2002. Minimum wage questionnaire. On-line at <http://www.gov.ns.ca/enla/>. Accessed Winter 2002. This questionnaire was quickly removed from the department's website and is no longer available.
2. Information gathered by fax and verified through a number of government and non-government sources, including Department of Training and Employment Development, New Brunswick, November 15, 2000; Nova Scotia Department of Environment and Labour—Labour Standards Division, November 15, 2000; Newfoundland and Labrador Department of Labour—Labour Standards Division, February 7, 2002; and Prince Edward Island Department of Community and Cultural Affairs, December 6, 2000.

Chapter 4

Creating Quiet Desperation

On Saturday, July 15, 2000, two newspapers in Atlantic Canada published front-page articles on the problem of panhandling. The Fredericton *Daily Gleaner* ran a story under the headline "Public too generous to panhandlers say police." An officer from the Fredericton city police force complained that regular fines were not an effective deterrent to panhandling because residents were too loose with their cash when confronted by panhandlers: "We're out issuing fines, but we're being told it's too lucrative for them [the panhandlers] to stop" (*Daily Gleaner* 2000: A1). It would appear that the problem of deterrence was being creatively managed in other Atlantic Canadian municipalities, however. On the same day the Halifax *Chronicle-Herald* (Pugsley-Fraser 2000: A1) reported that a local panhandler facing more than $20,000 in loitering fines might be thrown in jail. According to the article, a prosecutor for the Halifax Regional Municipality expressed the hope that the Haligonian would be jailed to work off the fines at the provincial rate of $44.80 per day. This would amount to an incarceration of 468 days. Readers learned that similar strategies of "default time" were successful in Dartmouth and that a similar case was under way in Bedford, Nova Scotia.

The articles share two underlying assumptions, which are broadly consistent with the neoliberal outlook on society. First, they assume that panhandling is a serious problem in Fredericton and Halifax, that the downtown cores of both cities are inundated with panhandlers who bother and harass local residents. Second, both articles indicate that the best solution to the problem of panhandling is to take legal aim at the panhandlers and get them off the streets through fines and incarceration. No other solutions are discussed, and the views of social activists and antipoverty workers are not offered. These articles promote the fashionable ideas that people who struggle with poverty in our society are a "problem" to be managed with efficiency and dispatch and that the managerial focus should be on laws and policies that target the behaviour of the poor themselves. Panhandling is not really a social problem but rather an individual problem; the challenge is to change the behaviour of the poor forcibly through a system of punishments and rewards.

Both articles are perfectly consistent with the temper of the age. In this neoliberal era society seems far less disposed to accepting responsibility for the challenges facing people who are forced to struggle in poverty. The qualification "seems" is important. There is a strong sense that people in Atlantic Canada are not in the habit of judging the poor very harshly. A Gallup poll from March 1998 found that Atlantic Canadians led all Canadians in charitable monetary donations and that only people in the prairie provinces donated more of their time—60 percent in the west compared with 58 percent in the east. It is worth remembering that the source of the problem according to the Fredericton police was the generosity of city dwellers; both the article and local law enforcement seemed determined to condemn panhandlers despite the fact that many residents seemed willing to pass along some of their spare change. One could reasonably suspect that the prevailing neoliberal temper of the age sits awkwardly against the spontaneous generosity of Atlantic Canadians.

Nevertheless, it is this judgmental outlook of officialdom that circulates in public commentary, even if it is difficult to gauge the degree to which these harsh assessments of the poor have settled in the minds of Atlantic Canadians. The climate of hostility in the neoliberal era is ironic. On one hand, neoliberal policies, especially those that have reduced the money going from the state to individual, have created even greater burdens for the poor. For a person who undertakes wage work irregularly, if at all, the opportunity to rely on social assistance as an alternative form of personal income has deteriorated considerably. On the other hand, neoliberalism cultivates a severely judgmental outlook on people struggling with poverty. In effect, neoliberalism intensifies poverty at the same time that it promotes a social outlook that harshly judges the poor; it attacks income supports and then attacks people who lack sufficient income. Harsh assessments of the poor were always latent in twentieth-century capitalism, but they have come to form an unchallenged wisdom that informs most of the social and political commentary of the last few decades. In the neoliberal era, questions about how society can eliminate poverty typically give way to questions about how best to manage the poor. The war on poverty is over; the war on the poor is well under way.

This double-edged assault on people struggling to eke out a living is not without a greater purpose. As outlined in this study, neoliberal policies have an inner logic related to the wage struggle. The attack on both income supports and the poorer people helps to maintain a glut of workers who are forced to assume low-wage positions throughout the economy. Strong income supports for workers who are either in employment transition or who may simply be down on their luck means greater job discretion as they search for work. And more tolerant public attitudes for those struggling in poverty place greater pressure on policy makers to provide meaningful social supports, supports that will provide real options for poorer people as they search for suitable employment. The neoliberal strategy of eating away at income supports is most evident in two areas, namely, unemployment insurance and welfare rates. It is implicitly recognized that a stronger unemployment insurance program and better welfare incomes combine to create greater job latitude for workers. Conversely, weak unemployment insurance programs and lower welfare rates create an expanded pool of potential low-wage workers. In a world singularly concerned with driving down the social wage, greater employment discretion for poor people on the margins of the economy is less palatable simply because it puts undue upward pressure on the low-wage sphere of jobs across the region.

Unemployment in Atlantic Canada

Remember EDS, the Texas-based company that officially announced that it was opening a call centre in Sydney, Nova Scotia, in the spring of 2000? Recall that the prime minister of Canada winged out to the east coast to participate in the announcement ceremonies and that local dignitaries joyfully proclaimed that the call centre was planning to create nine hundred jobs for Cape Bretoners. EDS is one of the leading technology companies in the United States, but the high-tech giant was then in the process of closing one of its call centre operations in Raleigh, North Carolina. According to the *Cape Breton Post* (2000: 4), EDS was experiencing considerable difficulty in maintaining its work force. Unemployment in the Raleigh area was around 1.2 percent, and local workers were voting with their feet by opting for better-paying jobs. In a relieved sort of way, the *Cape Breton Post* boasted that "workers aren't a problem in Cape Breton when unemployment rates often soar above 20 percent" (2000: 4).

This peculiar sentiment expressed in the local daily should be understood in context; this region has taken more than its fair share of hits in the era of globalization. In the grand sweep of capitalism unemployment is not such a bad thing, unless of course the unemployed decide to revolt against the system. A pool of reserve workers willing and able to step into capitalist workplaces helps to regularize production and keep wages depressed. Rather than raising wages at its Raleigh facility, EDS officials undoubtedly calculated that it would be much cheaper to relocate to an area where the supply of workers could be more or less guaranteed by the prevailing conditions of unemployment. The *Cape Breton Post* understandably was expressing the relief that jobs were about to be created in the Sydney area, but in fact the celebrated event was simply the matter of a large capitalist firm availing itself of a reserve pool of workers in a different region of North America.

Indeed, Atlantic Canada is a reserve pool of labour for North America,

Figure 4.1
Unemployment in Atlantic Canada

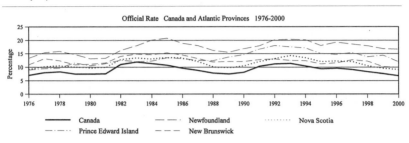

Source: Canada, Statistics Canada, CANSIM II

and this has allowed local governments to push for the establishment of call centres and other enterprises that are well known for their lower wages. Unemployment rates across Atlantic Canada are generally higher than those in the rest of Canada. As shown in Figure 4.1, between 1976 and 2000 the unemployment rate in each Atlantic Canadian province was always higher than the Canadian rate. The undulations in the unemployment rate across the region over the last twenty-five years are related directly to periods of stronger economic growth. However, the official rate of unemployment in the region rarely fell below 10 percent in any of the provinces. From the mid-1980s onward the unemployment rate in Newfoundland and Labrador exceeded 20 percent and never fell below 16 percent. Newfoundland and Labrador's rate was consistently higher than the other Atlantic Canadian provinces. In Prince Edward Island, the unemployment rate peaked at 18.1 percent in 1992 and never fell below 10.5 percent at any time in the last two decades of our survey period. The average rate of unemployment on the island in the 1990s was 15.8 percent. Nova Scotia posted the lowest unemployment rate in the region during the 1990s—9.6 percent at the close of the decade—although its average rate hovered around 12 percent over the same period. As Figure 4.1 shows, New Brunswick's unemployment tended to be the most stable across the region during the 1990s, ranging from 10.2 percent to 13 percent. Generally, unemployment rates in the Atlantic Canadian provinces were at least two percentage points above the Canadian average in any given year.

The official rate of unemployment is the one we are likely to encounter in the news, but this does not include many groups of people. When we take into consideration workers who have become discouraged, who are waiting to be recalled, who expect to start work more than five weeks down the line and who are not receiving the hours they would prefer, a much more comprehensive and accurate indication of the level of unemployment begins to emerge. We might refer to this as the real, or true, unemployment rate. As shown in Figure 4.2, the real unemployment rate

Figure 4.2
Real Unemployment in Atlantic Canada

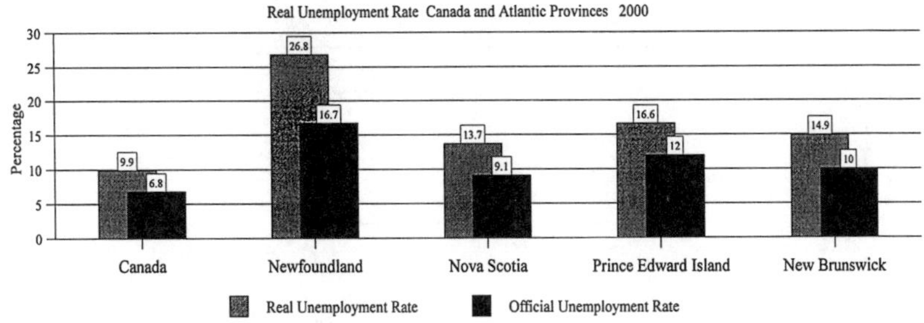

Real Unemployment Rate Canada and Atlantic Provinces 2000

Canada	Newfoundland	Nova Scotia	Prince Edward Island	New Brunswick
9.9 / 6.8	26.8 / 16.7	13.7 / 9.1	16.6 / 12	14.9 / 10

▨ Real Unemployment Rate   ■ Official Unemployment Rate

Source: Canada, Statistics Canada 2001

across Atlantic Canada was consistently higher than the official rate. Newfoundland and Labrador's real unemployment rate in 2000 was 26.8 percent, or about one in four people. Nova Scotia posted a real unemployment rate of 13.7 percent in 2000. The corresponding rate in Prince Edward Island was 16.6 percent, while the figure for New Brunswick was 14.9 percent. In every Atlantic Canadian province the real unemployment rate was at least four percentage points higher than the official rate.

Unemployment rates reflect the pool of workers who are potentially available for work. Although some of the unemployed in Atlantic Canada will step into high-paying jobs, a considerable number will undoubtedly be consigned to lower-wage jobs as they re-enter the work force. Adding to the pool of potential low-wage workers is invaluable from the standpoint of employers. The business community must be able to count on a supply of workers to fill positions in the lower-wage stratum. At this point, the challenge for governments is to ensure that the unemployed do not have meaningful income options, which would permit them to live with dignity while holding out for a higher-paying jobs.

In the neoliberal era the state has refined its technique of rolling the unemployed back into the work force as quickly as possible. This is most evident in the reforms to the unemployment insurance program in the early to mid-1990s. The government changed the name of the program to Employment Insurance to emphasize the employability of working people, but we'll continue to use the old language. Responding to pressure, the unemployment insurance system noticeably improved in the 1960s and 1970s. Benefits increased and coverage widened until the early part of the 1980s. This strengthening has been offset by its unmistakable decline in the last few years. Throughout the 1990s the unemployment insurance system deteriorated, especially for irregularly employed workers. Any general confidence that one could count on unemployment insurance earnings during rough periods or over the off-season has been severely

Figure 4.3
Deterioration of Unemployment Insurance for Atlantic Canadians

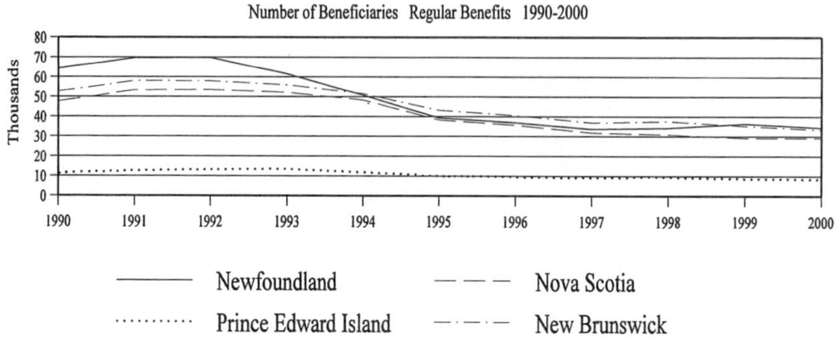

Number of Beneficiaries Regular Benefits 1990-2000

————— Newfoundland   — — — Nova Scotia

·············· Prince Edward Island   —·—·— New Brunswick

Source: Canada, Statistics Canada, CANSIM II

eroded. Roll-backs in the system began with Bill C-21, which was passed under the Tory regime in the early 1990s. Those reforms increased the number of weeks of work required to receive benefits and reduced benefit rates for those who declined "suitable employment," quit "without just cause" or were "fired." Three years later the federal government cut the regular benefit rate to 57 percent of insurable earnings. Even more significantly, in 1993 Bill C-113 completely eliminated coverage for workers who quit or were fired from their place of work. The Chrétien Liberals intensified this assault on the unemployment insurance system when they came to power. Changes introduced in 1994 cut benefits to 55 percent of insurable earnings, increased the number of weeks needed to qualify for benefits and decreased the benefit period for those who qualified.

The cumulative effect of this assault on the unemployment insurance system over the last decade has been extensive in Atlantic Canada. As depicted in Figure 4.3, despite the fact that unemployment rates have remained high across the region, the number of unemployment insurance beneficiaries dropped precipitously, especially after 1994. Although the number of beneficiaries are slightly affected by the overall growth rates of the economy, between the mid-1970s and the early 1990s there was a steady and gradual rise in monthly claims. Beginning in 1995, however, the number of beneficiaries began to fall off sharply. Workers were hardest hit in Newfoundland and Labrador, where the average number of monthly beneficiaries was more than 63,000 between 1990 and 1994 and less than 36,000 for the remainder of the decade, a decline of 43.3 percent. In 1992 the official unemployment rate in Newfoundland and Labrador was 20.2 percent and the average number of monthly unemployment insurance claimants was 69,727; in 1997, with the official unemployment rate still stuck at 18.6 percent, the average number of beneficiaries had fallen to 33,718, a decline of more than 50 percent. Comparable developments unfolded in the other provinces. Between 1990 and 1994, Nova Scotia averaged more than 50,000 claimants each month and just a little more than 32,000 over the remainder of the decade. New Brunswick experienced a corresponding decline of 32 percent over the same period, and the matching drop in Prince Edward Island was slightly more than 26 percent. Unemployment on the island stood at 17.6 percent in 1993, and there was an average number of 13,392 unemployment insurance beneficiaries in any given month of the year. Four years later the unemployment rate dropped slightly to 15.4 percent, but the average number of beneficiaries in any given month was just 9,227.

As one might anticipate, the clawback in the benefit rate of Employment Insurance meant that successful unemployment insurance beneficiaries in the late 1990s were receiving less income than their counterparts in the early 1990s. Importantly, the deterioration in income was usually greater than the lowered benefit rate, which reflects the general fact that benefits are tied to wages. Between 1992 and 2000, average weekly benefits for regular claims declined by 10.5 percent in Prince Edward Island, 8.4 percent in Newfoundland and Labrador, 8.0 percent in New Brunswick and 3.5 percent in Nova Scotia. In other words, the purchasing capacity of unemployment insurance benefits fell in every Atlantic Canadian province as the 1990s wore on.

The reforms to the unemployment insurance scheme has hit Atlantic Canadian workers especially hard, owing to the seasonal nature of much of the region's economy. The reforms to a program that was not strapped for cash can be explained only as a strategy to shuffle unemployed workers back into wage work as quickly as possible. The implicit goal of state policy is the maintenance of a glut of willing and able workers. In the areas of Atlantic Canada where seasonal economies combine with high rates of unemployment, greater numbers of workers will necessarily be thrown into the lower-wage economy. And even those workers who are able to receive unemployment insurance benefits will feel the pull of the low-wage economy as an option to their severely eroded incomes.

Poverty in Atlantic Canada

The United Nations declared 1996 the International Year for the Eradication of Poverty. According to a report by the National Council of Welfare (1998) in that same year poverty in Atlantic Canada was extensive. The rate of poverty for all persons ranged from 12.6 percent in Prince Edward Island up to 17.2 percent in Newfoundland and Labrador. At least one third of the region's single people were living in poverty, with rates of poverty as high as 37.1 percent in New Brunswick and 40.7 percent in Newfoundland and Labrador. Family poverty across the region was more

than 10 percent and more than 15 percent in Newfoundland and Labrador and Nova Scotia. Worse still, in 1996, child poverty stood at 16.8
percent in Prince Edward Island, 18.9 percent in New Brunswick, 22.5
percent in Nova Scotia and 24.7 percent in Newfoundland and Labrador.
In other words, roughly one in five Atlantic Canadian children were
living in poverty in the United Nation's special year devoted to its eradication.

The declaration of the United Nations was well received across the
region. In his Christmas address in 1995, the Lieutenant Governor of
Nova Scotia, John James Kinley, observed that the "United Nations has
designated 1996 as the Year of the Eradication of Poverty," and he enthusiastically endorsed it as "a truly laudable pursuit for all people and all
nations" (Kinley and Kinley 1995). Over the next year politicians in each
province echoed Kinley's lofty sentiments. For example, Joan Marie
Aylward, Minister of Social Services in Newfoundland and Labrador,
declared that October 17, 1996, would be recognized as the International
Day for the Eradication of Poverty in Newfoundland and Labrador.

Nevertheless, the region failed to respond to the spirit of the United
Nations campaign. Data from the National Council of Welfare (1999)
indicates that, by 1997, poverty had risen sharply across Atlantic Canada.
In Newfoundland and Labrador, the overall rate of poverty shot up from
17.2 percent in 1996 to 20 percent in 1997; the poverty rate for single
individuals rose from 40.7 percent to a staggering 51.3 percent, while the
rate of family poverty climbed to 17.7 percent from 16.6 percent a year
earlier. In Prince Edward Island the poverty rate for all persons rose to
13.3 percent, up from the 1996 rate of 12.6 percent, and the rates for single
people and families also rose over the same period. In Nova Scotia the
overall increase in poverty was less, although it still increased from 18.1
percent in 1996 to 18.5 percent in 1997, and the rate for single individuals
went up to 39.1 percent from 33.7 percent. In New Brunswick, the rate of
family poverty rose from 13.8 percent in 1996 to 14.8 percent in 1997,
although the province's overall rate of poverty remained unchanged at
15.8 percent. We can scarcely be surprised by the fact that two years later
the United Nations' Development Program's *Human Development Report*
(1999: 93) cited Canada for failing to reduce poverty and inequality.

As Table 4.1 reveals, the poverty rate across Atlantic Canada did not
improve significantly between 1980 and 1998. In Nova Scotia, the rate for
individuals increased from 16 percent to 17.4 percent. The rate for single
persons in New Brunswick stayed the same. The overall poverty rate in
Newfoundland and Labrador was down from 23.6 percent in 1980 to 19.8
percent in 1998, and the corresponding rate also dropped in Prince
Edward Island to 12.1 percent. Between 1980 and 1998, the rate of family
poverty fell by almost 5 percent in Newfoundland and Labrador and by
almost 3 percent in Prince Edward Island. Unfortunately, however, the

Table 4.1
Poverty Rates in Atlantic Canada, 1980–1998
Individuals, Families and Children

	1980	1982	1984	1986	1988	1990	1992	1994	1996	1998
Newfoundland and Labrador										
All individuals	23.6	21.4	23.0	22.0	16.6	15.6	20.0	19.1	17.2	19.8
Families	22.1	20.8	21.4	20.9	15.8	14.3	18.3	18.4	16.6	17.2
Children	26.2	24.4	27.1	23.8	20.0	19.6	25.4	23.5	20.0	24.5
Nova Scotia										
All individuals	16.0	18.8	17.7	16.4	14.2	13.4	17.2	17.0	18.1	17.4
Families	14.1	15.3	15.9	14.4	11.6	12.0	14.0	14.5	16.4	15.4
Children	15.0	20.9	19.4	17.8	14.2	16.5	19.7	20.2	23.7	21.2
Prince Edward Island										
All individuals	15.7	16.4	15.0	12.5	12.8	12.5	10.8	10.5	12.6	12.1
Families	12.1	14.3	11.8	8.8	10.6	10.2	7.5	7.9	10.6	9.2
Children	13.4	17.5	16.3	12.2	12.4	13.7	12.9	13.0	14.8	14.5
New Brunswick										
All individuals	16.9	21.5	21.3	16.1	14.6	14.3	13.8	15.5	15.8	16.8
Families	14.7	19.1	18.9	14.1	13.0	12.7	11.7	13.5	13.8	14.3
Children	18.2	25.4	25.7	18.0	16.8	17.1	15.5	18.5	19.6	20.2
Canada										
All individuals	15.3	16.4	18.1	16.0	14.8	14.6	16.1	16.6	17.6	17.2
Families	13.2	14.0	15.6	13.6	12.2	12.1	13.3	13.7	14.8	14.3
Children	14.9	17.8	19.6	17.0	15.4	16.9	18.2	19.1	20.9	19.6

Source: Adapted from National Council of Welfare, 2000c

family poverty rate rose in Nova Scotia from 14.1 percent in 1980 to 15.4 percent in 1998.

The last two decades showed some modest improvements across the region to be sure, but other trends dispel any optimism. When the matter of child poverty is considered an alarming picture emerges. In three of the four Atlantic provinces the rate of child poverty rose substantially in the 1980s and '90s. In Nova Scotia, the incidence of child poverty climbed from 15 percent in 1980 to 21.2 percent in 1998. New Brunswick recorded the next greatest increase, from 18.2 percent to 20.2 percent over the same period. In Prince Edward Island, the poverty rate rose from 13.4 percent in 1980 to 14.5 percent in 1998. Only Newfoundland and Labrador's disturbing rate of 26.2 percent in 1980 declined over the survey period, falling slightly to 24.5 percent in 1998 but remaining the highest rate of child poverty in Atlantic Canada.

When we focus on the 1990s an even more unsettling image of poverty begins to form. As shown in Figure 4.4, poverty rates across Atlantic Canada generally rose throughout the 1990s. Overall rates climbed in Nova Scotia from 13.4 percent in 1990 to 17.9 percent in 1998. In New-

Figure 4.4
Poverty Rates in Atlantic Canada, 1990–1998 #1

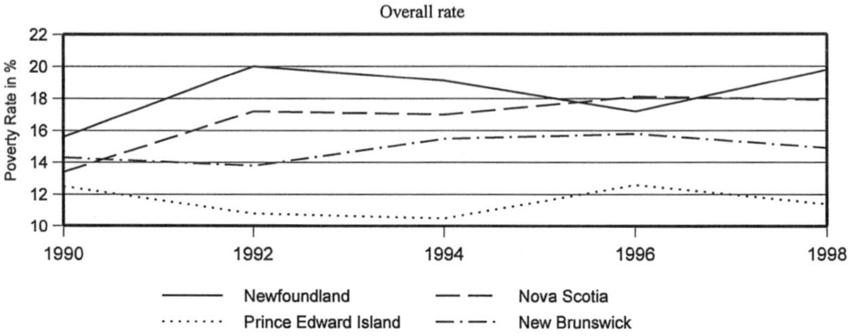

Source: Adapted from National Council of Welfare 2000c

foundland and Labrador, the overall rate rose from 15.6 percent in 1990 to 19.8 percent in 1998. The increase was just under 1 percent in New Brunswick. Only Prince Edward Island experienced a decrease in its overall rate of poverty during the 1990s.

After falling during much of the 1980s, the poverty rate for single persons also inched upwards in every Atlantic Canadian province during the 1990s. As shown in Figure 4.5, at the outset of the 1990s the rate for single persons soared from 27.6 percent in Nova Scotia to 43.6 percent in New Brunswick. Prince Edward Island's corresponding rate was 31.9 percent while Newfoundland and Labrador's stood at 38.9 percent. Over the next few years the poverty rate for single persons clearly worsened. In Newfoundland and Labrador, the rate shot up to 50.7 percent by 1998, an increase of 11.8 percent in just eight years. The increase in Nova Scotia was even more dispiriting; by 1998 the poverty rate for singles had climbed by 13.3 percent to stand at 40.9 percent. Smaller increases in the poverty rate for single persons were posted in the two remaining provinces. The rate rose in Prince Edward Island from 34.6 percent in 1990 to 37.4 percent in 1998 and in New Brunswick from 28.5 percent to 31.1 percent over the same period. As the 1990s drew to a close, roughly one in every three single persons in Atlantic Canada was living in poverty.

It would be difficult to sustain a claim that the war on poverty in Atlantic Canada made any appreciable headway over the last two decades. Poverty rates tended to undulate across the region during the 1980s and 1990s, falling modestly in some periods and rising noticeably in others, but they never displayed a strong and sustained downward movement. The modest exception to this trend was in Prince Edward Island, where the rates of poverty were down for all persons, families and children over our survey period. An inevitable question must be posed: Why does poverty persist in the region?

Figure 4.5
Poverty Rates in Atlantic Canada, 1990–1998 #2

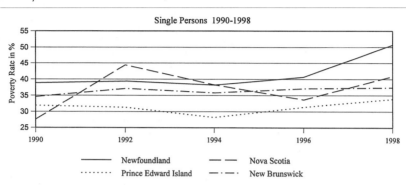

Source: *Adapted from National Council of Welfare 2000c*

At this point we must make an observation that adds to the imperative nature of our queries. Poverty is a problem with a rather simple and a relatively cheap solution. Governments could solve it with a modicum of political will. The National Council of Welfare's report on poverty in Canada in 1996 demonstrated that poverty generally was rising across the country, and it provided the dollar figures necessary to end it:

> Despite these grim realities, winning the war on poverty is not an unrealistic goal. Statistics Canada estimates that the cost of bringing all poor people out of poverty in 1996 would have been $17.8 billion. That's a huge, but not outrageous amount of money in a country where the federal, provincial and territorial governments spent $386 billion in 1996 and where the value of all the goods and services produced was $820 billion. (1998: 3)

In reporting on the year 1997, the council was even more direct in its claim that governments were not taking poverty seriously: "It is also crystal clear that most governments are not yet prepared to address these problems seriously, nor are they prepared to ensure a reasonable level of support for low-income people either inside or outside of the paid labour force" (National Council of Welfare 1999: 1). To put the matter baldly, politicians could throw money at poverty and the condition would be more or less alleviated. Even if politicians were unwilling to eradicate poverty via large injections of cash, we might at least expect to see a sustained decrease in poverty owing to improved social programs and government assistance of a less costly nature. Throughout the 1990s, however, poverty was on the rise in both Atlantic Canada and across the rest of the country.

Accounting for Poverty in Atlantic Canada

To understand why poverty persists in Atlantic Canada we must step back and reflect on the wider phenomenon of poverty in contemporary life. Poverty is not an accident of globalization. The central feature of our neoliberalizing world is the attack on the working class everywhere, and the goal is to drive down wages. Transnational capital has assumed the economic and political lead regarding wages, and the other factions of the corporate world are glad to follow suit. To this end, capital has restructured itself—downsized, relocated, outsourced and so on—to take advantage of cheaper labour in the South and to extract more from working people in the North. It has also aggressively promoted the neoliberal policy agenda—smaller governments, privatization, free trade, lower corporate taxes and cuts to social programs—to governments around the world. These strategies combine to encourage a downward pressure on all wages. When we consider globalization in terms of this elementary goal it is difficult to believe that it intends the widespread improvement of living standards. Indeed, rising poverty is a consequence of globalization and its real purpose.

At the level of human decency, poverty is a terrible thing. It destroys people. It robs them of their dignity, and in its most pernicious form it causes untold numbers to die. These harsh realities of poverty prompt many people to volunteer on behalf of families who are struggling with low incomes. Antipoverty groups have formed in many cities throughout Canada. Food banks have sprung up in most towns. Countless people put in time to run breakfast programs for local schools, organize food drives and volunteer at local shelters. Most of us find it very difficult to take poverty "in stride" as we might say.

Yet, if we adopt the perspective of the "business world," poverty suddenly becomes a much more tolerable thing. It goes hand-in-hand with what might be thought of as a wage dividend. Poverty forces people to take unpleasant, low-wage work. For many people around the world, the real choice is a rather stark one between insufficient access to the necessities of life or humiliating, low-wage employment. If capitalist societies provided a genuine option for people, if governments supported social programs so that the standard of living reached a socially acceptable level, jobless adults and their families would not be driven to accept poor working conditions and below-poverty wages. If the state was truly "there" for people, a manufacturer of appliances in Juarez, Mexico, or a coffee shop owner in St. John's would be forced to improve workplace conditions and raise wages to attract workers.

Why is poverty allowed to persist? Because it helps to sustain a pool of low-wage workers. No politician would admit this out loud, but political and economic elites across society intuit the advantage of impoverishment, and so it is encouraged. Of course, this contemporary equation between poverty and low-wage work presupposes the historical dispossession of most people from the earth, that is, from arable land. This ignoble aspect of capitalist history began with the land enclosures of England and continued until and after the Green Revolution in the Third World in the post-Second World War era. When people have access to land they have alternative ways to meet their basic needs on their own. They can live simply and proudly. Even in the not-too-distant past in Atlantic Canada one could find families and communities meeting many of their basic needs through both the cultivation and harvesting of small parcels of land and the bounty of the sea. Land dispossession forces people to find alternative means of survival. They have to find the money to purchase the necessities of life, and so they are drawn by necessity to the marketplaces of capitalism and to wage work. If the state were to help supply some of these basic necessities to those between jobs, effectively filling in the gaps created by the historic loss of land for families and communities, then the guaranteed supply of low-wage workers would begin to dry up. Our current social programs fail to lift individuals and families out of poverty, however, so our options in life are limited: either one accepts low wages and poor working conditions, or one suffers the ignominy of poverty. A distasteful conclusion is inescapable: in capitalist societies, poverty seems to be a tolerable thing insofar as it guarantees a continuous supply of people desperate enough to assume low-wage work.

To understand this argument we must understand the nature of daily life in poverty. Although statistics on poverty and unemployment paint an alarming picture, they do little to acquaint us with the day-to-day struggles that attend poverty. What is life like when one lives below the poverty line? Rare glimpses into the lives of those struggling with poverty have emerged in Atlantic Canada. In the spring of 1999, for example, the Cooper Institute in Charlottetown examined the lives of single mothers in the province. Its report entitled *Single Mothers: Surviving Below the Poverty Line* (Cooper Institute 1999) indicates the chronic difficulties and embarrassment associated with being poor.[1] Accepting a different standard of health care is common among the poor: "It is really distressing for me as a mother not to be able to save my teeth. When Social Services allow only extractions, it means that you have dentures at 30 years." Struggling to get adequate food is a fact of life as well. As one mother stated: "If I asked my worker to give me a list of nutritious food and I went to the store to buy them, the bill would be over what I could afford. It's very hard to afford meat on this budget. There are some things I can't buy for my little girl, like oranges." Parents commonly forego food for themselves to feed their children when income is lacking. "There are days," reported one mother, "when I just eat toast so that there will be food for my son. I get $550 a month from Social Assistance and $238 from CPP. I pay $510 for rent and have $278 to buy food and pay all bills." This daily struggle with insufficient income extends well beyond the home. "School programs are a headache. I can't afford it," lamented one mother, "the school asks for too much money from parents.... They are not geared to low income people. With the prices going up, I just can't afford it. It puts a lot of pressure on the kids." The onus is on the parents to devise strategies to avoid stigmatizing their children. This mother spoke of the stark trade-offs when faced with a lack of money:

> You don't have money for milk for the children. I was taking $65.00 out of my food money to buy lunches for the children. I can't continue. It makes me feel bad, discouraged. I keep my kids home when I can't give them lunches. Sometimes the oldest one stays home and I take his lunch and divide it for the two younger ones. I eat one meal a day. All day I live on coffee and tea. I am taking from me and my older child to feed the younger ones. I should be eating better ... but I can't afford to.

When one lives in poverty, each day is filled with anxiety and feelings of vulnerability. There is chronic stress, especially financial stress, at work and at home. Poverty means running out of money at the end of every month. Agonizing decisions need to be made, typically by women, between purchasing winter boots or school supplies rather than groceries. "Poverty Means," a poem written by Sharon Reese of Sussex, New Brunswick, (cited in National Anti-Poverty Organization 1996: 16) and presented at the Atlantic Canada Conference for Poor People in 1996, captures the daily grind of poverty best:

> Poverty Means
> Always having to say no.
> No, you can't go.
> No, you can't have.
> No, No, No.
>
> Poverty Means
> Endless line ups.
> At the Food Bank
> Line ups at the Welfare Office.
> Line ups, line ups, line ups.
>
> Poverty Means
> You are always waiting for the mailman.
>
> Poverty Means

You love every season of the year—
all but Winter.

Poverty Means
Never getting too attached to any of your
material possessions, you never know when you
will have to sell them in a yard sale.

The Role of the State in Maintaining Desperation

The challenge for the state is to maintain levels of social assistance that impel recipients and beneficiaries to seek employment or, as economists will say, enter the labour market. If rates of assistance are set too low, then the caring mythology of states and governments would be jeopardized and all the rhetoric about social safety nets would fly out the window. If rates are set too high, so that recipients and beneficiaries are permitted to live in dignity, then they would hold out for better jobs with respectable wages. Given the ideological temper of our age, we must always remember that poverty has nothing to do with laziness and everything to do with basic human dignity. The basic function of the state in this regard is to drive as many people as possible into the work force while avoiding public embarrassment and containing dissent.

These unwritten policies are most apparent when we examine welfare incomes, especially the welfare rates for single persons (also called "single employables"). It is this cohort of impoverished people that governments in Atlantic Canada—and, indeed, throughout the rest of the country—want to keep vulnerable. Consequently, welfare rates are set extremely low to drive them into the work force. These low rates have caught the attention of the National Council of Welfare. In a recent study of welfare incomes it concluded that,

> ... no province had welfare rates consistently closer to the poverty lines than elsewhere. Rates in some provinces, *especially rates for single employables*, are far below the lines. Welfare incomes which reach only one-fifth or one-third of the poverty line are unacceptably low and should be raised at the earliest possible date. (National Council of Welfare 2000b: 23; emphasis added)

In focussing on welfare rates for "single employables" the National Council of Welfare was merely drawing attention to the most glaring example of the general strategy of keeping welfare rates low across Canada and in the Atlantic provinces.

Figure 4.6 illustrates this aspect of the strategy to force single persons into the work force. In 1990, the rate of welfare income generated from

Figure 4.6
Welfare Income as Percentage of Poverty Line for Single Persons

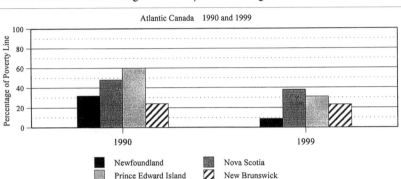

Source: Adapted from National Council of Welfare 2000b

provincial assistance programs and tax credits in each of the four Atlantic provinces left a recipient far below the poverty line, and the screws were turned even tighter as the decade wore on. In 1990, a single person receiving welfare in New Brunswick would have received only 24 percent of the income necessary to reach the poverty line, the lowest percentage across the region. In Newfoundland and Labrador a single person would have received 32 percent and in Nova Scotia 48 percent of the income necessary to reach the poverty line. The highest welfare income for a single person in 1990 was in Prince Edward Island, where one would have received about 60 percent of the necessary income to reach the poverty line. By 1999, the welfare incomes for single persons had fallen dramatically in three of the four provinces. As a percentage of the poverty line, welfare incomes in Newfoundland and Labrador plummeted from 32 percent in 1990 to just 9 percent in 1999. In Nova Scotia the corresponding measures fell from 48 percent to 31 percent, and in Prince Edward Island from 60 percent to 38 percent. In New Brunswick, welfare incomes for single persons held their ground, although they remained among the lowest in the region.

Figure 4.7 depicts provincial welfare rates for single persons in constant 1999 dollars. Rates nosedived in Newfoundland and Labrador, Nova Scotia and Prince Edward Island in the mid-1990s. The figure shows the sharpest declines in Newfoundland and Labrador, where welfare benefits over the course of a year amounted to $4599 in 1990 and just $1142 in 1999, a decline of more than 75 percent. In Prince Edward Island, rates fell from $8578 for single persons in 1990 to $5316 in 1999, a decline of almost 40 percent. The corresponding decline in Nova Scotia was 37.2 percent over the same period. Only New Brunswick had relatively stable welfare rates, but even there the decline was 7.9 percent.

Figure 4.7
Single Persons and Welfare in Atlantic Canada

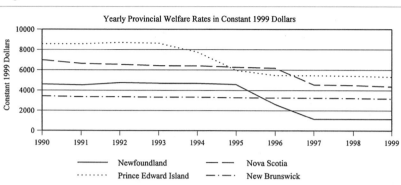

Yearly Provincial Welfare Rates in Constant 1999 Dollars

Legend:
——— Newfoundland   — — Nova Scotia
········ Prince Edward Island   — · — · New Brunswick

Source: Adapted from National Council of Welfare 2000b

It is clear that in Atlantic Canada a single person considered employable is forced into the labour market by punishingly low rates of social assistance. The lesson seems clear enough: work and live in poverty, or go on welfare and live in even greater poverty. In a region with its share of seasonal work, economies where workers might have a job with decent wages for at least part of the year, the options open to them in the "off-season" must seem unbearably bleak.

All social-assistance recipients are caught in the crossfire when it comes to the state's drive to maintain a pool of low-wage workers in Atlantic Canada. Many recipients who lack genuine employment options are harmed by these tacit standards and condemned to long periods of poverty. The National Council of Welfare (2000b: 25) reveals the following statistics for 1999. In Newfoundland and Labrador in 1999, a single parent with one child would have received only 70 percent of the necessary income to reach the poverty line. In Prince Edward Island, a similar family would have received only 60 percent of the necessary income. Welfare incomes are comparably insufficient for families in Nova Scotia and New Brunswick. These punitive transfers usually hit lone mothers, who lack any real employment options because of childcare responsibilities.

A similarly regrettable picture emerges when welfare transfers to disabled persons are considered in terms of the poverty line. In Newfoundland and Labrador, a disabled person would have received only 59 percent of the necessary income to reach the poverty line in 1999; this was down from 64 percent a decade earlier. In Prince Edward Island, a disabled person received only 59 percent of the income necessary to reach the poverty line in 1999, a disturbing decline of 15 percent in ten years. In Nova Scotia the corresponding figure for 1999 was 60 percent. In New

Brunswick, sadly, the figure falls to 47 percent, and even this was down from 63 percent in 1989. Even to the most hardened right-wing ideologue a person facing physical challenges must appear victimized by the punitive welfare incomes in Atlantic Canada.

When welfare incomes are considered alongside the attack on the working poor in Atlantic Canada it is easier to understand why a region that had less than 10 percent of the Canadian population in 2000 hosted almost 25 percent of the country's food banks (calculated from Wilson 2000). Understandably, the National Council of Welfare has chided provincial governments for failing to provide the bare necessities of life: "The fact is that the [poverty] cut-offs already represent very low levels of income. The only 'discretion' many welfare recipients have is to cut back on food when the money starts running short toward the end of the month" (2000a: 36). The National Anti-Poverty Organization's *Welfare Report Card*, was even more direct:

> The dominant ideology of our time seems to put more and more emphasis on the market place, with minimal government intervention to protect the interests of the poor and to ensure the provision of access to basic services as a matter of right rather than ability to pay. At some point, however, there will inevitably be a backlash against this trend. History shows that democratic societies which fail to maintain a balance between social justice and individual liberty are at risk of losing basic civic and human rights.[2]

Attacking the Poor Rather than Poverty

Despite the efforts of governments to roll people out of the poverty of welfare and into the "respectable" poverty of low-wage jobs, poverty persists, and it is an embarrassment to economic and political elites. To minimize this unease Canadian officialdom has shifted its outlook on poverty—the war against poverty has become a war on the poor themselves. At one time poverty was treated as a "social question," a social problem requiring government and community action. Over the last two decades, however, this has given way to the downloading of blame onto the poor themselves. A phenomenon of "poorism" has rooted itself in the everyday language of society and politics. People struggling with poverty are routinely profiled by neoliberal elites and their intellectual disciples; they are accused of not having the outlook and drive suitable to the new global economy. Poor bashing has become commonplace. A pernicious idea wafts over the neoliberal countryside: "The poor are poor largely through their own fault."

As the casualties of globalization mount, it is ironic that the very idea of social responsibility has been withering. In the new climate, society, as such, is not to be blamed for someone's disappointments or dire circumstances. Governments are now in the business of attributing a person's hardship or struggles in our globalizing world to his or her personal failings. Commentators remind people that prosperity may be around the corner but that, in the meantime, sacrifices have to be made. Politicians admonish the public to "live within its means." Working people are told to tighten their belts and to be thankful for the jobs they have. There has been a revival of the notion of the rugged individual who must be flexible and able to adapt to the new economy, who must respond to new challenges and who must be open to a "hand up" rather than a "hand-out." Indeed, the intellectual attendants of neoliberalism have invented new ways to hurl abuse at the poor. A brief survey of some of the public commentary and circulars from the Atlantic Institute for Market Studies (AIMS) reveals that harsh judgments against people struggling with poverty are circulating across Atlantic Canada. In one AIMS commentary, an explicit distinction is made between child poverty and other types of poverty. On the matter of child poverty, its author is unequivocal: "Child poverty is a terrible thing. If you're like me, the notion of children living in our midst, without the basic necessities of life, is morally abhorrent and politically unacceptable" (Crowley 1997). So far, so good. Almost immediately, however, the author begins to attack the claim that upwards of one in four children in Canada are living in poverty; politicians and "professional advocates for the social welfare industry" are accused of "grossly misrepresenting the real state of child poverty in this country." Claims about child poverty, we learn, are "exaggerations" that come from the "intellectually dishonest use of Statistics Canada data." The AIMS author stresses that commentators are employing the word "poverty" when they really should be speaking of "income inequality"—a very different matter that is open to much more disagreement within policy-making circles and, indeed, across society.

So let us pause for a moment. If we ignore the accusations that politicians pander on behalf of the poor (a very peculiar idea in the neoliberal era) and that those who work tirelessly on behalf of the poor exaggerate the facts to keep their jobs (more often than not a volunteer position), is it possible that we are merely encountering a dispute about how best to characterize a nagging social problem? Are we speaking of poverty or income inequality? If so, it would be inappropriate to suggest that AIMS' concern for poor children conceals its promotion of its free market agenda, although the gratuitous attacks on antipoverty workers would surely make anyone suspicious. We may ask: Why is a neoliberal policy institute like AIMS concerned about child poverty? When its broader outlook is examined, an answer to this question is forthcoming. AIMS makes a simple distinction between child poverty and adult poverty. In the words of its president (Crowley 1997): "In the case of adults in poverty, one can always ask to what extent their actions have contributed to their state. Children are by definition dependent. There is no moral ambiguity about their poverty." This distinction permits AIMS to assign blame to adults struggling with poverty. In a recent speech to the Federal Finance Senior Officials' Retreat in May 2001 (Crowley 2001), the head of AIMS was clear about the extent to which the adult poor should be judged. There are two kinds of poor, he said; those who pass through poverty relatively quickly, and those who remain stuck in poverty for periods exceeding a year. The first group is not a concern:

> The first class are not especially problematic for social policy, but note why: they have ingrained in them a set of behaviours and expectations, including discipline and a sense of the value of work, which allows them to move relatively easily out of low income and back into a way of life more in keeping with their expectations. The turnover in this class of the poor is just one sign of the robustness of the particular individuals that find themselves there at any particular moment. (Crowley 2001)

As for the second class of adult poor, however, things are a different matter entirely. According to the president of AIMS:

> Contrary to much political rhetoric and the claims of the welfare rights movement, poverty is not merely—or even primarily—an economic condition. It is also in many cases a cultural condition—it involves values. That means that poverty can never be overcome by mere income support or the passive writing of cheques, but only by challenging and changing behaviour. Poverty really is a question of character to a surprising extent. (Crowley 2001)

The speech went on to claim that the poor think only in terms of the here-and-now. They lack the belief that "investments do pay off." In practical terms, they do not equate work with long-term prosperity and independence:

> [I]f it is true that some people work hard and escape poverty, then many of those left behind could also have escaped, but did not— not necessarily because they are lazy, but rather because they may lack the set of cultural values which make success possible. (Crowley 2001)

At this point everything is out on the table. Many poor are not "necessarily lazy" but rather, well, unmotivated. Somewhat predictably, the speech concluded that the privatization of welfare services across Canada is the best way to wean the poor off social assistance. In the end, the poor are not poor because they were born poor, because they are challenged with a disability, because they are a single parent of young children, because they are attached to a region facing chronically high unemployment, because they cannot stand the humiliation of another degrading job with rotten wages, because work is seasonal, because they are separated from their partner, because of long-term illness within the family or because their wages are too low. Rather, they lack sufficient motivation. The connotative distance between "insufficient motivation" and "laziness" is not great, although the first expression would appear to be more pleasing to neoliberal ears.

This severely judgmental line of argumentation perpetuates certain stereotypes about the poor. Unfortunately, politicians so frequently parrot these attacks on the poor that the expression "poor bashing" has entered our everyday lexicon. Even at its best, the response of politicians to poverty, while rhetorically empathetic, lacks any sincere commitment to reducing poverty. The contention of this study is that expressions of concern about poverty by politicians, government officials and business leaders are largely insincere. In electoral democracies where politicians are careful not to alienate particular constituencies, where political aggregation and platform-blending constitute the golden rule, it is simply "good politics" to express concern about poverty and the poor, at least for the most part. However, these political affectations belie a lack of sustained concern and attention, as well as inadequate efforts to ameliorate poverty across Atlantic Canada and across the country. Expressing concern for poverty makes for a good "sound bite," but politicians quickly learn that it makes for bad public policy.

Of course, we do occasionally find politicians who take an active interest in poverty. Former Canadian Senator Erminie Joy Cohen of Saint John has often expressed the kind of authentic concerns that politicians can come to possess, and her personal account of her enlightenment about poverty is revealing:

> In the spring of 1996, I was invited to be the Honourary Chair of the Atlantic Canada Conference for Poor People, "Voices in Action," being held in Saint John, New Brunswick, my home city.... I attended that conference with notes in hand and a genuine sense of pride that I might be viewed as a sympathetic "dignitary" to the plight of the poor. What I experienced during that conference profoundly altered the context in which I viewed my world. In the midst of this gathering of people of poor economic status, I was moved by the wealth of spirit that was expressed in

their dignified and honest discussion about being poor in Canada. I was both shocked and inspired by that conference, and I was determined to add my voice and my resources as a Senator to the quest to sensitize Canadians and governments to the true state of poverty in Canada today. I strongly believe that those with influence, be they elected or citizens at large, need to hear the truth about being poor from those who live in poverty to better understand how poverty affects us all. (Cohen 1997: vii)

As part of this commitment the senator from Saint John produced two studies on poverty within three years. Her 1997 report entitled *Sounding the Alarm: Poverty in Canada* provided a wide-ranging review of poverty in Canada and formulated a direct attack on the neoliberal agenda:

In the 25 years since the Croll Report entitled *Poverty in Canada* was published, the face of poverty in our country has aged, not gracefully or with dignity, but through deprivation and hardship, hastened in part by government policies that do not reflect a real understanding of the social or political consequences of poverty. Why else do we see social programs under continual attack, with the most vulnerable in society bearing the burden of debt and deficit reduction? (Cohen 1997: vii)

Three years later Cohen co-chaired the Progressive Conservative National Caucus Task Force on Poverty, which included New Brunswick Members of Parliament Gilles Bernier from Tobique-Mactaquac and Jean Dubé from Madawaska-Restigouche. The report of the task force stresses that poverty continues to be a debilitating problem across Canada:

While we certainly gained a realistic perspective and learned a great deal from poor people and the groups that are working to improve their lives, much of the testimony supported what Canadians and their governments should already know: that poverty is worsening, not in a time of recession, but in a time of economic growth. The hearings validated what we knew intuitively: there is a persistent and growing gap between the rich and the poor in Canada, a gap which is growing larger and more pervasive.... Information about the extent and growth of poverty in Canada and its dire consequences has been available for years, thanks to the important research that has been done by antipoverty organizations, community groups, government bodies and academics. (Progressive Conservative National Caucus Task Force on Poverty 2000: ii)

Both of the reports spearheaded by Senator Cohen contain a sweeping survey of poverty in Canada and both reports reject the narrow right-wing measures of poverty characteristic of the Atlantic Institute for Market Studies:

> Absolute poverty, or the calculated cost of keeping a human being alive, is determined by adding up the cost of food, shelter and clothing. Personal care allowance, transportation requirements, child care, health care beyond essential services, reading materials, and school supplies are not taken into account. It is not difficult to understand the purpose of such a poverty measure to those trying to wrestle dollars away from social programs. They want to convince government and the people of Canada that the poor can survive on less—much less—than the current welfare rates. (Cohen 1997: 3)

Although the 2000 report of the Progressive Conservative National Caucus is more cautious and politically restrained than the 1997 report by Senator Cohen, and although the second report appears to water down Cohen's earlier efforts, Cohen's commitment and sincerity regarding poverty has not been diminished. It is an exception among politicians. Most politicians have been leading public denunciations of the poor, demonizing them and vilifying them for daring to "live off" government hand-outs. In the context of the debt panic, politicians argue that annual deficits are due to excessive spending on social programs, directly implicating the poor in the fiscal woes of the Canadian state. Edna Doiron, a National Anti-Poverty Organization board member living in New Brunswick, summarized this trend well:

> Welfare recipients are blamed for the debt of society, pointed out at every opportunity, labeled and discriminated against. Poor bashing has become an acceptable way of life.... People in poverty are called cheats, abusers, lazy. How many times have you heard someone say they know of someone on welfare who's abusing the system? At times, it would appear the government would have you believe everyone that relies on welfare is an abuser. When the accusations are started, it takes little coaxing for people to believe it and little time before fingers are being pointed and name calling begins, and hatred spreads. (Doiron 1998: 4)

A tiering system has developed between the deserving poor and the undeserving poor. And in everyday political discussions, the working poor are less contemptible than the slothful poor who receive social assistance.

Conclusion

In May 1996 the city of Saint John, New Brunswick, hosted *Voices in Action: Atlantic Canada Conference for Poor People* (National Anti-Poverty Association 1996). The four-day conference included workshops, seminars and talks devoted to enhancing public understanding about poverty. One theme of the conference addressed the harsh assessments that are made of the poor. Issues such as "poornography" (using negative stories about poor people to inflame judgments about the poor) and "poor bashing" were raised repeatedly throughout the weekend. One conference workshop corrected the prevailing misunderstanding succinctly: "Being poor is a circumstance, not a reflection of character" (National Anti-Poverty Organization 1996: 12–13). In understanding the prevailing tendency to judge the poor harshly, however, we must also acknowledge that this tendency is hardly accidental.

Notes

1. The following five quotations are from *Surviving Below the Poverty Line* (Cooper Institute 1999).
2. This quotation was available on the National Anti-Poverty Organization's website and was accessed in January 2002 at < http://web.archive.org/web/20010214051521/www.napo-onap.ca/naporeport.htm >. Immediately prior to the publishing of this book, NAPO's site was under construction. NAPO has confirmed the quotation by telephone, however.

Chapter 5

The Gathering Politics of Globalization

The Manufacture of Austerity

In the early spring of 2000 the New Brunswick Minister of Finance Norman Betts stood before members of the provincial legislature to deliver the first provincial budget of the new century (Betts 2000). Before any of the details of the budget were announced New Brunswickers learned that the budget would be balanced. The finance minister stressed that the new government's accounting procedures were "clear and open," that it was "managing smarter" and that it was "focussing on public priorities" (Betts 2000: 5–6). The new Conservative regime was emphasizing honest accounting, and Betts relayed a story about his great-grandfather and the importance he had placed on plain and open accounting practices:

> Mr. Speaker, as I deliver my inaugural budget speech, I am reminded of the first budget speech given by my great-grandfather, Robert Murray, who served as New Brunswick's provincial secretary-treasurer from 1917 to 1920. Mr. Murray said he would present "a simple, frank, straightforward and comprehensive statement which portrayed the financial position of the province in a fuller and more complete manner than had those of preceding administrations for some years past." Today, we are also presenting a balanced budget that reflects a straightforward portrayal of the Province's financial position. (2000: 6)

Concern about vague accounting procedures loomed large in the early years of the Lord government, concerns that have been publicly promoted by the far right across Canada, especially by the Fraser Institute. It was clear that the finance minister was not about to be accused of obscurantism when it came to the province's bookkeeping.

Open accounting was not really the concern driving the new government's agenda, however. The goal, as the finance minister honestly stated at the outset of his budget speech, was to balance the budget. The call for stricter accounting practices generated a heightened awareness of fiscal errors in the province's past. The new recording procedures for debts, New Brunswickers learned, meant that the estimated 1998–1999 surplus of $18.5 million was really a deficit of $164.3 million (Betts 2000: 7). And so the provincial debt had really increased. The government was not about to let this trend continue: "Mr. Speaker, looking ahead, the situation would get worse, not better. If this trend were to continue, New Brunswick would find itself in a precarious fiscal position characterized by a widening gap between expenditures and revenues" (Betts 2000: 7). The finance minister then delivered a sobering post-mortem on the twilight of Keynesianism in the province: "From 1988 ... to 1999 total expenditures have increased by an annual average compound growth rate of 2.6 percent while revenues have grown at an average annual compound growth rate of 2.4 percent" (Betts 2000: 7). The alarming message could now be delivered without equivocation:

> The real picture is beginning to take shape. Expenses are growing faster than income. Borrowing has increased to make up the difference. Contributions from federal transfers have been reduced. Gross debt and debt service costs are climbing. When you combine these factors, the result is a serious financial problem for the province. If left unchecked, New Brunswick taxpayers would face annual deficits of close to half a billion dollars within four years. (Betts 2000: 8)

Concerns that previous governments had "cooked the books" became a way to justify new policies of austerity. The revised assessment of the province's finances permitted the Lord government to hammer home a message about the need for restraint in the era of globalization. The government admitted that it had to make some tough decisions:

> To correct this problem, this government has had to focus on priorities, and make choices. Do we fund health care or corporate welfare? Do we invest in more books for school children or more bureaucracy for government? Do we cut taxes or create more programs? ... Mr. Speaker, we know that New Brunswickers will never choose more deficits and more debt. (Betts 2000: 8)

And so spending was not about to increase dramatically despite the presence of a "real" balanced budget for the first time in recent memory:

> In an environment where there is no blank cheque, the dialogue

with government officials and citizens was not about spending more. Instead it was about how to better use available government, financial, human and community resources to achieve a cohesive vision of social development. (Betts 2000: 8)

The conclusion of the new finance minister's inaugural budget address reiterated the familiar message of debt discipline and austerity:

Very simply, the message is this—New Brunswick is at a crossroads and there is a choice of directions we can take. We can choose as a province to continue down a well-worn path of deficits and debt, or we can choose a new path that will lead New Brunswick to fiscal, economic, and social success. (Betts 2000: 29)

The tenor of the Lord government's first budget was entirely in keeping with the message of restraint of the last two decades, even if its approach was a little more creative. The job of governments in Atlantic Canada in recent years has been to deliver the message of austerity. In a world where working people have been struggling with anxieties about their future, rising expectations would be politically and socially dangerous, and governments understand this all too well. And so prosperity will come only through the attentive application of neoliberal policies—and it will always be down the road. Most importantly, governments are now out of the business of spending their way to prosperity. The manipulative presentation of the matter of public debt in the last twenty years has served governments well by giving them an excuse to slash and burn. Belts have to be tightened. People have to make sacrifices. Provinces have to develop their strengths. Keynesianism is dead. In an address to the Metropolitan Halifax Chamber of Commerce in November 1999, Nova Scotia Premier John Hamm stated: "Why is deficit-financing wrong? What are the consequences? I said a moment ago that government can't create prosperity—at least they can't create the kind of prosperity that lasts. But they can destroy it."[1]

One of the clearest paths to fiscal maturity and austerity was marked out in Prince Edward Island during the 1990s. During the formative years of debt hysteria the outlook was decidedly less draconian on the island than in the rest of the country. In 1990, for example, Provincial Treasurer Gilbert Clements boasted to the legislature that the province already had its "fiscal house in order," although he expressed grave concern that the federal government was about to download some of its debt management onto the province by cutting transfer payments: "One would hope that our province would not be fiscally burdened by a transfer of the federal deficit due to our ability to better manage our affairs" (1990: 12). As steep federal cuts became a reality and therewith created fiscal chaos on the island, a more caring and sensitive tone was evident in Clements's 1992 budget:

> It [the budget] could have followed the example of previous administrations and other jurisdictions and cut or eliminated a number of programs and services. This action would have addressed in a seemingly effective and clinical manner, Mr. Speaker, the "numbers problem".... However, it also would have created job losses in both the private sectors and the public sectors, and damaged this government's mission to provide a full range of necessary social programs for Islanders. Instead, Mr. Speaker, our government has approached the financial difficulties in a socially humane and rational manner. (1992: 1)

Over the next few years, however, the process of rationalizing the rollbacks went into full swing. Clements's successor, Wayne Cheverie, spoke about a turning point in the province's financial affairs and expressed grave concern about the size of government. In 1995, as the severity of the cuts was becoming evident to everyone, Cheverie spoke of his journey from youthful idealism to fiscal realism:

> I am reminded of another time in my career as an elected representative and Minister of the Crown, when the central preoccupation of government was in broadening the human social services to Islanders, and when the spectre of deficit and debt did not loom over our heads. In fact, Madame Speaker, if I might digress here for a moment, I came into public life in 1986 full of energy and optimism, as a self-professed social reformer.... [M]y first ministerial assignment was in the portfolios of Justice, Labour and Housing. I very much enjoyed these responsibilities. (Cheverie 1995: 1–2)

After reminding everyone that no minister can "escape budgetary responsibility," he spoke of his trepidation when he was offered the Treasury portfolio in light of his social idealism:

> I must tell you and other Members of the Assembly, Madame Speaker, that in all honesty I was personally unsuited and probably ill-prepared in April of 1993 when the Premier asked me to serve as Provincial Treasurer. And certainly, after becoming fully informed about the financial situation confronting us at that time, I did wonder if I had the heart for the job. However, I also realized that even in the face of such an unprecedented problem of escalating deficits and diminishing federal revenues, I was

being called on to do what was right, in spite of the sacrifice and pain that would be involved for many. (Cheverie 1995: 2)

Cheverie's heartfelt sojourn into fiscal adulthood was complete. The choice for him, in the face of dismal fiscal realities, was a clear one between the idealism of youthful naiveté and responsible behaviour:

> We could have avoided the grim reality, and placed blame on others, and allowed the deficit to spiral upward, taking with it much of our financial independence. But what a price to pay, and what a future to leave our children. There was no alternative at all. And therefore with mixed emotions, but with determination, government faced up to its responsibilities and implemented radical expenditure reduction measures designed to achieve financial stability. (Cheverie 1995: 4)

Cheverie's path to fiscal enlightenment has been taken, sometimes reluctantly, sometimes enthusiastically, by all Atlantic Canadian politicians and, indeed, by all Canadian politicians in the last two decades.

On the Other Side

The neoliberal agenda has not gone unchallenged. Opponents have written letters of protest, held study sessions, established research centres to confront the claims of neoliberal supporters, worked in soup kitchens and food banks, organized protests and marches, prepared and circulated leaflets and flyers, actively supported more sympathetic political candidates and parties, established organizations to help the poor, altered their consumption habits, honked as they have driven past weary strikers and walked picket lines.

These confrontations with neoliberalism have been sustained over a period of two decades, and they usually depend on the volunteer work of countless individuals who remain skeptical and wary of the prevailing political messages of the day. In Atlantic Canada these efforts have frequently coalesced around the production of alternative provincial budgets. These budgets challenge the main assumptions of neoliberal governments and recommend spending alternatives premised on well-being and inclusive social development.

A brief examination of the 1998–1999 alternative provincial budget for Prince Edward Island, a province with an impressive and inspiring antipoverty community, will provide us with a better sense of what such documents entail. The island's alternative provincial budget was produced in April 1998 through the support of a wide range of groups, including the Cooper Institute, the MacKillop Centre for Social Justice,

Miminegash Women in Support of Fishing, the Canadian Union of Public Employees, the Council of Canadians, the University of Prince Edward Island Student Council, the provincial Federation of Labour, the provincial Teacher's Federation, the Canadian Catholic Organization for Development and Peace and the Action Canada Network. It was written by a number of islanders, including long-time antipoverty activists Mary Boyd and Brian Curley. The efforts were coordinated by the Prince Edward Island (PEI) Action Canada Network, and the alternative budget itself was published by *Street Feat: The Voice of the Poor,* Atlantic Canada's first "street" newspaper. In the words of the budget itself:

> The Prince Edward Island Alternative Budget Working Group is composed of several active Island groups working under the umbrella of the PEI Action Canada Network. These include social justice, anti-poverty, teachers, farmers, fishers, women's groups, church groups, labour, interested individuals and people with inside experience of the workings of government, including academics. This is our first attempt to examine aspects of the provincial budget in order to address the basic and urgent needs of Island residents from all walks of life, but especially those who have been excluded and marginalized. (PEI Action Canada Network 1998: 2)

It stresses the reality of life for some on the island as opposed to the popularized image of the island nationally and internationally:

> Although the citizens of Prince Edward Island are proud of their province and many non-islanders, certainly at first glance, consider it to be an idyllic place where everybody lives in peace, harmony and relative prosperity, there are basic and chronic problems in our society. (PEI Action Canada Network 1998: 2)

The opening paragraphs of the alternative budget establish the political tone of the document, emphasizing that a "corporate model" of government harms many people in Prince Edward Island:

> In recent years the government and its agencies have adopted a corporate model of governance. While there is an abundant debate as to the effectiveness of this model for business, it is certainly not the correct model for government, the elected body which is obliged to fulfil a role of safeguarding the common good of society, including the provision of adequate safety nets, adequate health care and other basic necessities. We believe that the present political and economic system works against the overall

good of society and therefore requires transformation to allow for urgently needed change. (PEI Action Canada Network 1998: 2)

The alternative budget provides commentary on many of the issues facing island residents, including video lottery terminals, the unequal distribution of wealth and power, child poverty, the low minimum wage, the lack of equal opportunity and unemployment. Importantly, it directly attacks government-created debt hysteria and the cultivation of a culture of austerity in the province:

> We believe that the majority of Island residents have been hurt by the hype surrounding debt and deficits. Yet, our governments continue to portray an inability to view money spent in health, education, environmental protection, adequate welfare and job creation as an asset rather than a liability. This mentality has led to cutbacks and suffering. Furthermore, provincial governments continue to fall for the myth that social programs, rather than tax avoidance, low corporate taxes and high interest rates, are the cause of the deficit. (PEI Action Canada Network 1998: 2)

Prince Edward Island's alternative budget made a number of general recommendations for rebuilding the province's economic infrastructure, renewing the social infrastructure and strengthening the island's culture. Specific recommendations ranged from improved housing and better job creation programs to greater support for public education and the healthcare system. In arguing that the political system is aloof to many islanders, and calling for the people to exercise greater control over government policy, the budget demonstrates analytical directness and political courage, especially considering the province's reputation for bald-faced patronage and political favouritism:

> Our present political system requires little commitment to the people. Years of policy-making that favours a small elite have led to a disastrous deterioration of the economic situation of the majority, while improving conditions for a privileged minority, thus ever widening the gap between rich and poor.... In order to ensure that the PEI government will truly act in the interests of the people and therefore rise above the ever present temptation to reward friends, we suggest holding public hearings aimed at truly dialoguing with all segments of the population about ways to improve the democratic process.... Year in and year out, government after government continues to escalate the growing gap between the rich and poor. (PEI Action Canada Network 1998: 11, 8)

To solve this problem the alternative budget calls for grass-roots political reform:

> A process of extensive discussion at the community level must be undertaken to help find a more effective political system, one that suits the realities of our times and functions in a truly democratic way. A discussion on this topic is in itself educating. Feedback by non-vested interests about how governments can begin to perform effectively the job they were elected to do on behalf of the people, is long overdue. Therefore, let us initiate an open, public discussion and exposure of the system. (PEI Action Canada Network 1998: 2)

The island's alternative budget is a testament to the indefatigable efforts of those who oppose the neoliberal agenda. Yet, like the provincial budgets across the region, it fails to locate the challenges facing residents of Prince Edward Island in the broader context of globalization. It is an effort rich with noble sentiments about the need for greater democracy, for governments to be accountable to the people and for just social policy. To this extent, it provides a powerful counter to neoliberal doctrine in the province. In centring its critique on democratic ideals and vague notions of "the people" and in failing to locate its agenda in the context of globalization, particularly globalization's direct attack on working people in Prince Edward Island and around the world, however, the alternative budget jeopardizes its potential political impact. Globalization is not about attacking democracies, nor does it take aim at "the people." Rather, it embraces any form of government that promotes its agenda, and it attacks *working* people. Globalization is not populist; it is classist. The alternative budget in Prince Edward Island reveals a strength and courage that cannot be trivialized. Yet, its language and its restrictive analytical setting reveals a fundamental challenge facing the movement against neoliberal policies in Atlantic Canada and, indeed, across Canada.

Atlantic Canada and the Politics of Globalization

When we scrutinize the political character of globalization a peculiarity emerges. We can elaborate on this peculiarity by drawing upon a common aphorism of politics and power: "Where there is power, there is resistance." Michel Foucault made this observation in *The History of Sexuality*, and it is probably one of the great insights of the twentieth century. Resistance does not always evolve into concerted political struggle, however. Globalization bears this distinction out unequivocally. There is an immature character or feel to the politics of globalization in Canada. One senses a political latency that is not quite manifest.[2] Political force is fully developed on one side only—the side of capital. For working people, the political struggle remains fragmented and disaggregated. The *class struggle* in the era of globalization is dynamic and robust, but the *class politics* of globalization are irregular, vague and, at times, almost absent from the course of public life.

Certainly we see aspects of the class struggle all around us. Working people regularly refuse dangerous tasks, file grievances, work to rule, strike, protest and, occasionally, occupy factories. Indeed, wage earners have few illusions about the unfair character of the capitalist workplace. The elementary suspicion among working people that the laws of the land are stacked against them has undoubtedly intensified in recent years, contributing to a general malaise. There is a timeless struggle—a class struggle—centred in and around the workplaces of capitalism, which consumes managers and workers alike. In the era of globalization this struggle has intensified as managers and owners strive to gain the upper hand in a political climate generally hostile to working people.

In spite of its robustness, however, this class struggle, rooted in the basic character of capitalism and intensified in the era of globalization, has not materialized with the same clarity at the level of politics. Political expressions of working-class interests are irregular and intermittent. A sustained class politics is conspicuously absent from contemporary Canadian politics. The interests of working people are commonly voiced by trade unions, labour federations, research centres, antipoverty organizations, progressive coalitions and so forth, but they do not coalesce into permanent—that is, sustained, widespread, coordinated—political action. There is no political struggle that corresponds to and reflects in intensity and scope the class struggle unfolding at the level of the workplace. Transnational capital has pitted itself against working people around the world, and, although working people and their allies have resisted this attack in innumerable ways, their acts of resistance have yet to fuse into a coherent force that resists the predations of its class foe on the political plane. Instead, transnational capital confronts a misshapen coalition that fundamentally misreads the character of globalization and its assault on working people around the world. A war is afoot, a class war, but the martinets have shown up only on one side. We have class struggle or, perhaps better class "resistance," but the class politics of globalization are, as one might say, "underripe."

Is this distinction between class struggle and class politics in the era of globalization overdrawn? More importantly perhaps, is it unfair to encourage this distinction in view of the tireless efforts of so many people who actively campaign against globalization in all of its forms? Many of these efforts have been applied in the Atlantic Canadian region, as is evident in everything from the production of alternative budgets to the consumption of "fair trade" coffee. But what do these efforts mean politically? Do they translate into sustained political pressure on behalf of working people? Are the interests of working people appropriately centred and elaborated by these struggles? Do the politics of globalization correspond to the main players of globalization? To what extent are the political interests of working people compromised by the mixed bag of issues that defines the progressive left—the antiglobalization left—in Canada? These are different questions to be sure, but the query is guided by a basic concern: Do we see the emergence of a political force that addresses the essential nature of the attack on working people in Canada and around the world?

To explore the claim that the politics of globalization have only a fledgling or immature character, we can compare the politics of transnational capital and the politics of the antiglobalization movement using three distinct criteria: the clarity of their respective agendas; the character of their respective agendas; and the degree to which their ideas are culturally suffused.

Clarity of the Agenda

The agenda of transnational capital is clear and precise: to relentlessly promote the goal of lowering production costs by lowering labour costs. To this end it has exalted the principle of free markets around the world. Accordingly, it attacks anything that is perceived to interfere with the operation of free markets, including labour laws, protectionist trade policies, regulation, taxation burdens, environmental restrictions, social assistance policies and state-run economic activities. This policy vision is promulgated at every turn. Institutes and economic think-tanks have been set up around the world to get the free-market message into public circulation and to insure that all factions of capital share this outlook, at least rhetorically. "Free marketism" is a simple idea that responds to the straightforward imperative to lower wages. In the idea of free markets transnational capital has found a principle that doubles as a slogan. Its political achievements are quite impressive.

In contrast, the agenda of the antiglobalization movement is amorphous and open-ended. A dizzying array of goals is pushed. We encounter calls for stronger environmental protections and for greater accountability to "the people" with respect to the practices of supercorporations and international trade organizations.[3] Sometimes we witness petty nationalist ideas being bandied around, with particular attention given to the preservation of Canada.[4] Attention is afforded to the erosion of social programs, aboriginal rights, safeguards for the poor, the promotion of civil rights and so forth.[5] Many of these agendas end up colliding with each other, as for example when the rights of workers are pitted against the need to protect the environment. Indeed, the antiglobalization movement often champions what may be described as "benign" globalization, a position that fails utterly to appreciate the real historical point of globalization, namely, the relentless drive to reduce labour costs.

The antiglobalization agenda coheres only by virtue of a vague sense of social injustice or political unfairness. It loses sight of the driving motive behind globalization, and its political ambiguity sits awkwardly against the logical and consistent guiding principles of transnational capital and the precision of its assault on workers. The antiglobalization agenda lacks a working-class centre; no singular, worker-friendly, organizing principle—say "the dignity of working people"—guides its outlook. Cynically put, the antiglobalization agenda is a flexible agenda perfectly in keeping with the era of flexible production. It is, in colloquial speech, "all over the place," even as international capital targets working people relentlessly. Although it might be a very unpopular idea to express, it is nonetheless true that a progressive agenda is not quite the same thing as an agenda set for working people. The point is not to find the right slogan but to address the absence of an appropriate political focus for the antiglobalization movement. Since globalization is about extracting more surplus value out of working people around the world, the organizing principle of the antiglobalization movement should reflect this.

Agenda Control

The political agenda is set by transnational capital. When we survey the leading policy issues in Canada over the last twenty years—free trade, the Goods and Services Tax, government debt, the size of government, privatization of public corporations, deregulation of the economy, the reform of federal and provincial social programs, etc.—it is important to understand that they have been the bailiwick of transnational capital. The Business Council on National Issues has set the political agenda in Canada, as have its counterparts in the rest of the world. Only the "Quebec question" lies outside of this profound influence; and, of course, the member corporations of the Business Council on National Issues are largely indifferent to the matter since Quebec would opt out of Canada long before it would opt out of the global neoliberal order, including the North American Free Trade Agreement. As this agenda has pressed forward it has given rise to newer issues, such as the fate of Canadian health care, but the agenda itself largely has been set by an alliance between the heads of industry and political elites across the country.

The antiglobalization movement plays no role in the setting of the national political agenda. It is entirely reactionary. The progressive left has been trying the stem the neoliberal tide, and it measures its success by its ability to forestall the disintegration of one social program after another. More often than not it merely responds to the policy preferences of transnational capital and fails to promote its own political vision, particularly one centred around working people and their aspirations. It is not surprising then that transnational capital has been largely unfazed by its political efforts. When successful, the antiglobalization movement acts as a drag on the forward press of neoliberal reforms—"the great roll-back," as we have been saying in this study. The neoliberal order has been constructed in an incremental fashion over decades, and this drag effect is not to be trivialized in any way. Nevertheless, in the political sense, stemming the neoliberal tide is nostalgic and defensive, and the working-class agenda remains peripheral to the course of daily politics across the country. The progressive left plays little determinative role in the course of Canadian politics. It is not so much that there is a collision of agendas in Canadian politics, but rather a prevailing neoliberal agenda coexisting with greater or lesser degrees of dissatisfaction, resistance and criticism.

Political Suffusion

Neoliberal thinking is everywhere. In recent years it has come to form a journalistic common sense, the everyday wisdom that guides most discussions about public policy across the country. Its alluring language of efficiency, responsible state spending, flexibility and free markets has been absorbed effortlessly into the intellectual horizons of politicians, journalists, academics, bureaucrats and, indeed, even many on the left. Neoliberal standards have burned themselves into the political consciousness of the vast majority of political and media elites across the country. It has become the unchallenged policy code that guides intellectuals and decision makers from the municipal to the federal level. In short, neoliberal ideas now form an unrivaled policy framework throughout Canada.

In dramatic contrast, the antiglobalization outlook enjoys no such status. Worker-friendly ideas appear at the margins of public discourse in Canada. Indeed, they are often condemned as antiquated, especially when worker-friendly policies are linked to state spending. The worker's story is not the guiding narrative of political and social commentary anywhere in Canada, and concern for the innumerable victims of globalization often appears as an afterthought. The prevailing concern in public life is for the economy—that is, profits—and concern about the well-being of people often seems rhetorical and insincere.

The agenda of transnational capital is extensively institutionalized in Canada. It is embedded in the state, in the leading political parties at federal and provincial levels and in international institutions such as the International Monetary Fund or the World Trade Organization. The radical free-market agenda structures the policy conduct of these bodies. Moreover, Liberal, Conservative, Alliance and New Democratic Party platforms across Canada are subordinated to neoliberal principles with modest variations in degree. In contrast, the antiglobalization agenda largely is external to the formal political structures in Canada. The interests and claims of working people have very little meaningful bureaucratic presence in the leading institutions of the Canadian state or in the country's leading political parties.

Of course, many research groups, labour federations and individuals promote the interests of working people, but they are more or less exterior to the policy-making process and the formal structures of power. Indeed, in the neoliberal world they can be discredited as "special interests," accorded the same status as local philately societies. Worse still, the antiglobalization movement must abide by rules of the state, rules that dramatically narrow its range of options. Indeed, at times the movement is judged according to vague standards about civil responsibility and democratic propriety, standards that smother options and quell spontaneous dissent against "the system." Clearly, the antiglobalization movement is on the outside, looking in on the formal operations of state power.

The Gathering Politics of Globalization?

After surveying these three criteria we reiterate the claim that the politics of globalization are insufficiently formed. A fully developed political force led by transnational capital runs up against a very fragmented opposition that lacks political cohesion and decisiveness. More to the point, the collision between opposing forces at the political level fails to reflect the nature of the collision between opposing forces that essentially defines globalization. Globalization, broadly conceived, is a contest between transnational capital and working people; but at a more narrowly conceived, political level, transnational capital meets a progressive political movement that responds insufficiently to the concerted attack on working people. Political programs centred around "the people" miss the basic point of globalization. Transnational capital has not targeted "the people"; rather, it has taken aim at "working" people. This is more than another plea for the revival of a genuine politics of class against a vague sort of left-wing populism, and it does not mean that causes important to everyone on the left need to be discarded. Rather, it means recognizing that the pluralist character of the left in Canada in the era of globalization has been politically devastating and that it has short-changed the working class. It is not a matter of anyone stepping back, but rather of labour leaders stepping up. Nero ought not to have fiddled while Rome burned.

The political forces in contention with global capital have yet to congeal, due to the lack of a clear political centre to respond to the essential point of globalization—the attack on working people—and working people pay for this blunder each day. A core political principle in keeping with the rudimentary character of globalization is desperately needed. The forces for working people in Canada will do well to note that in April 2002 hundreds of thousands of Italians engaged in a general strike and demonstrated across the country to protest against a law that would have made it easier to fire workers. They shut down the country. Such a massive worker-centred disruption, organized by Italy's leading trade unions and premised so clearly on issues relating to the power of working people, particularly conservative Prime Minister Silvio Berlusconi's vow to reform labour laws, is telling and illuminating. The politics of globalization in Canada could mature in time, but there is ground to cover.

For the moment, we continue to suffer through all manner of ideologically loaded claims and boasts about globalization. We see radiant appraisals of globalization as a glorious step forward for humankind. We are told that globalization will allow nations to take advantage of their unique traditions and economic strengths, bring prosperity and leisure to more people, promote a more cosmopolitan world, foster unparalleled technological innovation, encourage the flowering of democracy and freedom and bring an end to the evils of the last two centuries. Peter Schwartz and Peter Leyden write in the "The Long Boom: A History of the Future, 1980–2020," a fictional retrospective on the global economy, which received considerable attention after it appeared on-line in *Wired Magazine* in the summer of 1999:

> We are watching the beginnings of a global economic boom on a scale never experienced before. We have entered a period of sustained growth that could eventually double the world's economy every dozen years and bring increasing prosperity for— quite literally—billions of people on the planet. We are riding the early waves of a 25-year run of a greatly expanding economy that will do much to solve seemingly intractable problems like poverty and to ease tensions throughout the world. And we'll do it without blowing the lid off the environment.

Unfortunately, such ideological commentary is completely indifferent to the facts. We are more than twenty years into Schwartz and Leyden's "global economic boom," and it is impossible to find evidence of "increasing prosperity" in Atlantic Canada. Across the region working people have faced greater difficulties and lost political and economic ground. Rates of unionization have stagnated; working-class confidence has been eroded; wages are deteriorating; labour laws have atrophied and are just as likely to be used against working people as on behalf of them; the minimum wage has fallen precipitously, with many jobs across the region clumping around this miserable baseline wage; women are forced to assume a disproportionate number of low-wage jobs; the unemployment insurance regime has been gutted; and rates of poverty are not abating.

The best of all possible worlds? Hardly. The fledgling politics of globalization in Canada cannot mature too soon.

Notes

1. This quotation is from a copy of the premier's State of the Province Address, delivered November 15, 1999.
2. This assessment does not share the optimism of other commentaries from the analytical left, cautious though they may be. For example, see Tabb 2000.
3. I take this to be the basic point of Rebick 2000, although it is a very popular standpoint.
4. The tireless work of the Council of Canadians stands out in this regard (see Clarke and Barlow 1997), although these views are equally common within the academy. For example, see McBride and Shields 1997.
5. Groups supporting these efforts range widely and include the Canadian Council on Social Development and the Canadian Council of Welfare.

Bibliography

Atlantic Provinces Economic Council. 2000. "Forty Billion Dollars Worth of Major Projects Helping Atlantic Canada to Build for the Future." Press release. July 12.

Bates, Robert H. 2001. *Prosperity and Violence: The Political Economy of Development.* New York, NY: Norton.

Betts, Norman. 2000. *Changing Our Future Together: Budget Speech.* Fredericton, NB: Government of New Brunswick, Department of Finance.

Black, Jan Knippers, ed. 1999. *Inequity in the Global Village: Recycled Rhetoric and Disposable People.* West Hartford, CT: Kumarian.

Bourdieu, Pierre. 1998. *Acts of Resistance: Against the Tyranny of the Market.* New York, NY: New.

Brac de la Perriere, Robert. 2000. *Brave New Seeds: The Threat of GM Crops to Farmers.* Halifax, NS: Fernwood.

Burgoyne, Arthur G. 1971. *Homestead: A Complete History of the Struggle Between the Carnegie Steel Company and the Amalgamated Association of Iron and Steel Workers, July 1892.* New York, NY: A.M. Kelly.

Canada, Statistics Canada. *CANSIM II: Canadian Socio-economic Information Management System* [database]. Ottawa: ON: Statistics Canada [producer and distributor]. August 2002.

_____. *Labour Force Historical Review: Labour Force Survey 2001* [CD-Rom]. Ottawa, ON: Statistics Canada [producer and distributor].

_____. 2000. "Recent Trends in Provincial Gross Domestic Product." *Canadian Economic Observer.* December: 3.1–3.7. Ottawa, ON: Minister of Industry.

_____. 2001. *Low Income Cut-offs from 1991 to 2000.* Cat. no. 75F0002MIE-01007. November. Ottawa, ON: Statistics Canada.

Cape Breton Post [Sydney, NS]. 2000. "Workforce Gets a Chance." Comment section. April 1.

Cayo, Don. 1999. "Low Taxes Better than Higher Minimum Wage." June 21. On-line at <http://www.aims.ca/Media/1999/prjun2199.htm>. Accessed September 12, 2002.

Cheverie, Wayne D. 1995. *The Budget Address.* Charlottetown, PE: Government of Prince Edward Island, Provincial Treasury.

Clarke, Tony, and Maude Barlow. 1997. *MAI: The Multilateral Agreement on Investment and the Threat to Canadian Sovereignty.* Toronto, ON: Stoddart.

Clements, Gilbert R. 1990. *Budget Speech and Estimates.* Charlottetown, PE: Government of Prince Edward Island, Provincial Treasury.

_____. 1992. *Budget Speech and Estimates.* Charlottetown, PE: Government of Prince Edward Island, Provincial Treasury.

Cohen, Erminie Joy (with Angela Petten). 1997. *Sounding the Alarm: Poverty in Canada.* Ottawa, ON: n.p.

Comish, Shaun. 1993. *The Westray Tragedy: A Miner's Story.* Halifax, NS: Fernwood.

Cooper Institute. 1999. *Single Mothers: Surviving Below the Poverty Line.* Charlottetown, PE: Cooper Institute.

Crowley, Brian Lee. 1997. "Coming to Grips with Child Poverty." *AIMS Commentary.* May 12. On-line at <http://www.aims.ca/Archive/commentary/12-597.html>. Accessed September 25, 2002.

_____. 2001. "Social Policy in the New Economy." Comments to Federal Finance Senior Officials' Retreat. Cornwall, ON. May 23. On-line at <http://www.aims.ca/commentary/fedfinance.htm>. Accessed September 12, 2002.

Daily Gleaner [Fredericton, NB]. 2000. "Public Too Generous to Panhandlers Say Police." July 15.

Danford, Andy. 1997. "The 'New Industrial Relations' and Class Struggle in the 1990s." *Capital and Class* 61 (Spring): 107–41.

Dobbin, Murray. 1998. *The Myth of the Good Corporate Citizen: Democracy Under the Rule of Big Business.* Toronto, ON: Stoddart.

Doiron, Edna. 1998. "Poor and Poverty." *NAPO News* 63 (March): 4. Ottawa, ON: National Anti-Poverty Organization.

Duménil, Gérard, Mark Glick, and José Rangel. 1985. "The Tendency of the Rate of Profit to Fall in the United States." *Contemporary Marxism* 11 (Fall): 138–52.

Foster, John Bellamy. 2000. "Monopoly Capital at the Turn of the Millennium." *Monthly Review* 51: 11 (April): 1–18.

Fox, Bonnie, and Pamela Sugiman. 1999. "Flexible Work, Flexible Workers: The Restructuring of Clerical Work in a Large Telecommunications Company." *Studies in Political Economy* 60 (Autumn): 59–84.

Fraser Institute. 1999. "Minimum Wage Equals Minimum Opportunity." News release. February 9. Vancouver: Fraser Institute. On-line at <http://oldfraser.lexi.net/media/media_releases/1999/19990209.html>. Accessed September 12, 2002.

Gallup Canada. 1998. *Canadians Show Volunteering Spirit.* March 13. Toronto, ON: Gallup.

_____. 1999. *Unemployment Remains Atop List of National Concerns with Healthcare a Close Second.* February 10. Toronto, ON: Gallup.

Gill, Stephen. 1990. *American Hegemony and the Trilateral Commission.* Cambridge: Cambridge University Press.

Government of Newfoundland and Labrador, Department of Environment and Labour. 1999. "Government Increases Minimum Wage." News release. March 22. On-line at <http://www.gov.nf.ca/releases/1999/envlab/0322n16.htm>. Accessed September 25, 2002.

Government of Nova Scotia, Department of Labour. 1996. "Minimum Wage Changes." News release. May 7. On-line at <http://www.gov.ns.ca/cmns/msrv/nr-1996/nr96-05/96050709.htm>. Accessed September 12, 2002.

_____. 1997. "Minimum Wage Reminder." News release. January 30. On-line at <http://www.gov.ns.ca/cmns/msrv/nr-1997/nr97-01/97013002.htm.> Accessed September 25, 2002.

Government of Nova Scotia, Sydney Steel Corporation. 2000. "Province Paying Out Sysco Credit Lines: Sydney Steel Corporation." News release. March 31. On-line at <http://www.gov.ns.ca/news/details.asp?id=20000331006>. Accessed September 25, 2002.

Government of Prince Edward Island. 1999. "Minimum Wage Amendment." News release. September 21. On-line at <http://www.gov.pe.ca/news/getrelease.php3?number=1279>. Accessed September 12, 2002.

GPI-Atlantic. 2001. *Income Distribution in Nova Scotia.* July 18. On-line at <http://www.gpiatlantic.org/pubs.shtml>. Accessed September 12, 2002.

Graham, Monica. 1998. "Committee Hears Tales of Economic Hardship." *Chronicle-Herald* [Halifax, NS]. October 5.

Gray, Anne. 1998. "New Labour—New Labour Discipline." *Capital and Class* 65 (Summer): 1–8.

Greider, William. 1997. *One World, Ready or Not: The Manic Logic of Global Capitalism.* New York, NY: Touchstone.

Hamm, John F. 2000. *State of the Province Address.* Metropolitan Halifax Chamber of Commerce, Halifax, NS. November 1. On-line at <http://www.gov.ns.ca/prem/speeches/state1_11_2000.htm>. Accessed September 12, 2002.

Harrod, Jeffrey. 1987. *Power, Production, and the Unprotected Worker.* New York, NY: Columbia University Press.

Heron, Craig. 1989. *The Canadian Labour Movement: A Short History.* Toronto, ON: Lorimer.

Human Resources and Development Canada, Workplace Information Directorate [Ottawa, ON]. 2001. Telephone interviews and email to author. May.

Huws, Ursula. 1999. "Material World: The Myth of the 'Weightless Economy.'" In *The Socialist Register* edited by Leo Panitch and Colin Leys. London: Merlin.

Kapstein, Ethan B. 1999. *Sharing the Wealth: Workers and the World Economy.* New York, NY: Norton.

Kinley, John James, and Grace Elizabeth Kinley. 1995. "Lieutenant Governor—Holiday Season Message: 1995 Holiday Season Message by Their Honours, Hon. John James Kinley, Lieutenant Governor of Nova Scotia, and Mrs. Grace Elizabeth Kinley, Government House, Halifax." News release. December 15. On-line at <http://www.gov.ns.ca/cmns/msrv/nr-1995/nr95-12/95121503.htm>. Accessed September 25, 2002.

Korten, David C. 1995. *When Corporations Rule the World.* West Hartford, CT: Kumarian.

Lacey, Kevin. 1996. "Making Labour Markets Work: *AIMS Commentary.* The Wage Trap: The Politics of the Minimum Wage." *The Beacon* 2 (Summer). On-line at <http://www.aims.ca/Archive/Beacon/1996/wage.html>. Accessed September 12, 2002.

LaFeber, Walter. 1999. *Michael Jordan and the New Global Capitalism.* New York, NY: Norton.

Lasch, Christopher. 1995. *The Revolt of the Elites and the Betrayal of Democracy.* New York, NY: Norton.

Law, Marc. T. 1999. "The Economics of Minimum Wage Laws." *Public Policy Sources* 14. On-line at <http://oldfraser.lexi.net/publications/pps/14/>. Accessed September 12, 2002.

Laxer, James. 1999. *The Undeclared War: Class Conflict in the Age of Cyber Capitalism.* Toronto, ON: Penguin.

Lord, Bernard. 2000. "Speaking notes for Premier Bernard Lord." Premier's IT Forum. Mactaquac Inn. Fredericton, NB. October 3. On-line at <http://www.gnb.ca/0089/speeches-discours/forum.htm>. Accessed September 12, 2002.

MacDonald, Tanya Collier. 2000a. "Call Centre Helps Reduce Province's Burden: Premier." *Cape Breton Post* April 1.

_____. 2000b. "It's Official: 900 Jobs for Sydney: Prime Minister's Visit Proves Beneficial for Cape Breton." *Cape Breton Post* April 1.

Mander, Jerry. 1978. *Four Arguments for the Elimination of Television*. New York, NY: Morrow.

Martin, Hans-Peter, and Harald Schumann. 1996. *The Global Trap: Globalization and the Assault on Democracy and Prosperity*. Montreal: Black Rose.

Marx, Karl. 1964. *The Economic and Philosophic Manuscripts of 1844*. New York, NY: International.

_____. 1976. *The German Ideology*. Moscow: Progress.

McBride, Stephen, and John Shields. 1997. *Dismantling a Nation: The Transition to Corporate Rule in Canada*. Halifax, NS: Fernwood.

McQuaig, Linda. 1998. *The Cult of Impotence: Selling the Myth of Powerlessness in the Global Economy*. Toronto, ON: Viking.

Mill, John Stuart. 1994. *Principles of Political Economy*. Oxford: Oxford University Press.

National Anti-Poverty Organization. 1996. *Voices in Action! Atlantic Canada Conference for Poor People*. Saint John, NB. May 16–19. Ottawa, ON: National Anti-Poverty Organization.

_____. 1998a. *Poverty and the Canadian Welfare State: A Report Card*. Ottawa, ON: National Anti-Poverty Organization. On-line at http://web.archive.org/web/20010214051521/www.napo-onap.ca/naporeport.htm. Accessed January 2002.

_____. 1998b. *NAPO News* 63 (March). Ottawa, ON: National Anti-Poverty Organization.

National Council of Welfare. 1998. *Poverty Profile, 1996*. Ottawa: Public Works and Government Services Canada.

_____. 1999. *Poverty Profile, 1997*. Ottawa: Public Works and Government Services Canada.

_____. 2000a. *Welfare Incomes, 1997 and 1998*. Ottawa: Public Works and Government Services Canada.

_____. 2000b. *Welfare Incomes, 1999*. Ottawa: Public Works and Government Services Canada.

_____. 2000c. *Poverty Profile, 1998*. Ottawa: Public Works and Government Services Canada.

New Brunswick, Newfoundland and Labrador, Nova Scotia and Prince Edward Island Federations of Labour. 1994. *Make It Fair: The Campaign*. Ottawa, ON: Canadian Labour Congress.

Petras, James, and Henry Veltmeyer. 2001. *Globalization Unmasked: Imperialism in the 21st Century*. Halifax, NS: Fernwood.

Prince Edward Island Action Canada Network. 1998. *Alternative Provincial Budget*. Charlottetown, PE: Street Feat.

Prince Edward Island Legislative Assembly. 1994. *Prince Edward Island Acts*. Ch. 32, sect. 10, p. 213–14. Charlottetown: Queen's Printer.

Progressive Conservative National Caucus Task Force on Poverty. 2000. *It's Up to*

Us! Report of the Progressive Conservative National Caucus Task Force on Poverty. January.

Pugsley-Fraser, Amy. 2000. "Panhandler Facing Jail Over Fines." *Chronicle-Herald* [Halifax, NS]. July 15: A1.

Rebick, Judy. 2000. *Imagine Democracy.* Toronto, ON: Stoddart.

Rinehart, James. 1998. "Transcending Taylorism and Fordism? Two Decades of Work Restructuring." In *Work, Difference and Social Change: Two Decades after Braverman's Labour and Monopoly Capital.* Conference proceedings. May 8–10. State University of New York, Binghamton, New York.

Sanga, Dimitri. 2000. "Income Inequalities within Provinces." *Perspectives on Labour and Income* 12 (4): 33–38.

Schellenberg, Grant, and David P. Ross. 1997. *Left Poor by the Market: A Look at Family Poverty and Earnings.* Social Research Series, Paper no. 2. Ottawa, ON: Centre for International Statistics at the Canadian Council on Social Development.

Schwartz, Peter, and Peter Leyden. 1997."The Long Boom: A History of the Future, 1980–2020." *Wired Magazine* 5.07 (July). On-line at <http://www.wired.com/wired/archive/5.07/longboom.html>. Accessed September 12, 2002.

Shutt, Harry. 2001. *A New Democracy: Alternatives to a Bankrupt World Order.* Halifax, NS: Fernwood.

Smith, Tony. 1994. "Flexible Production and the Capital/Wage Labour Relation in Manufacturing." *Capital and Class* 53 (Summer): 29–63.

Steuter, Erin, and Geoff Martin. 2000. "The Myth of the Competitive Challenge: The Irving Oil Refinery Strike, 1994–1996, and the Canadian Petroleum Industry," *Studies in Political Economy,* 63 (Autumn): 111–32.

Swift, Jamie. 1995. *Wheel of Fortune: Work and Life in the Age of Falling Expectations.* Toronto, ON: Between the Lines.

Tabb, William K. 2000. "After Seattle: Understanding the Politics of Globalization." *Monthly Review* 51: 10 (March): 1–18.

Taylor, Frederick Winslow. 1998. *The Principles of Scientific Management.* Don Mills, ON: Dover.

Teeple, Gary. 2000. *Globalization and the Decline of Social Reform: Into the Twenty-First Century.* Toronto, ON: Garamond.

Telegraph Journal [Saint John, NB]. 1998. "Foodbank Use in Atlantic Canada Double the Rest of the Country." September 18.

United Nations Development Programme. 1999. *Human Development Report: Globalization with a Human Face.* On-line at <http://hdr.undp.org/reports/global/1999/en/>. Accessed September 26, 2002.

Wilson, Beth. 2000. *Hungercount 2000: A Surplus of Hunger.* Toronto, ON: Canadian Association of Food Banks.

Index

Global Issues Series ...

co-published by Fernwood Publishing and Zed Books

Related Titles from Fernwood Publishing

Paradigm Shift: Globalization and the Canadian State
Stephen McBride
160pp ISBN:1-55266-061-3 $19.95

RESIST! A Grassroots Collection of Stories, Poetry, Photos and Analysis from the FTAA Protests in Québec City and Beyond
Jen Chang, Bethany Or, Eloginy Tharmendran, Emmie Tsumura, Steve Daniels & Darryl Leroux, eds.
192pp ISBN:1-55266-063-X $19.95

Bringing the Food Economy Home:
Local Alternatives to Global Agribusiness
Helena Norberg-Hodge, Todd Merrifield & Steven Gorelick
co -published by Kumarian Press 172pp ISBN:1-55266-082-6 $19.95

Globalization Unmasked: Imperialism in the 21st Century
James Petras & Henry Veltmeyer
co-published by Zed Books 224pp ISBN:1-55266-049-4 $24.95

Inside Capitalism: An Introduction to Political Economy
Paul Phillips
285pp ISBN:1-55266-104-0 $29.95

Protest and Globalisation:
Prospects for Transnational Solidarity
James Goodman, ed.
co-published by Pluto Press Australia 275pp ISBN:1-55266-085-0 $28.95

The Globalisation Decade: A Critical Reader
Leo Panitch & Colin Leys, eds.
co-published by Merlin Press 260pp ISBN:1-55266-088-5 $24.95

The Impasse of Modernity:
Debating the Future of the Global Market Economy
Christian Comelieu
co-published by Zed Books 192pp ISBN:1-55266-068-0 $19.95

The Three Waves of Globalization:
A History of a Developing Global Consciousness
Robbie Robertson
co-published by Zed Books 288pp ISBN:1-55266-100-8 $29.95